FIVE FUNDAMENTALS

FIVE
FUNDAMENTALS

◆

STEVE ELKINGTON
Reveals the Secrets of the Best Swing in Golf

with Curt Sampson

BALLANTINE BOOKS ◆ NEW YORK

A Ballantine Book
Published by The Ballantine Publishing Group

Copyright © 1998 by Steve Elkington

All rights reserved under International and Pan-American Copyright Conventions.
Published in the United States by The Ballantine Publishing Group,
a division of Random House, Inc., New York, and simultaneously in
Canada by Random House of Canada Limited, Toronto.

http://www.randomhouse.com/BB/

Library of Congress Cataloging-in-Publication Data
Elkington, Steve.
Five fundamentals: Steve Elkington reveals the secrets of
the best swing in golf / Steve Elkington with Curt Sampson.
        p.   cm.
ISBN 0-345-42152-3 (alk. paper)
1. Swing (Golf).   2. Golf.   I. Sampson, Curt.   II. Title.
GV979.S9E45   1998
796.352'3—DC21   98-19534
                                                    CIP

Text design by Debbie Glasserman

Manufactured in the United States of America

First Edition: November 1998

10 9 8 7 6 5 4 3 2 1

CONTENTS

NOTE TO THE READER

*F*IVE *FUNDAMENTALS* CONTAINS four swing sequences to flip through, giving the reader a chance to see Steve Elkington's swing in action. Simply grasp the pages and flip them from the front of the book to the back. The first sequences show two views of Steve's swing with the driver: from the caddie's view, at the top of the page, and from behind Steve, at the bottom of the page. On page 107, the sequences change: at the top of the page, to the six-iron as seen from behind, and at the bottom of the page, to the sand bunker shot as seen from the caddie's view. These sequences should give you a feel for the smooth tempo that has led Steve Elkington to be named as possessor of the best swing on Tour four years in a row.

INTRODUCTION

Steve and Lisa Elkington and their two young children live in a sunny neighborhood in North Houston, with giant oaks and pines sheltering broad, green lawns and mansions of brick. The Elkingtons have the biggest trees on the block—no, in the state—and landscaping that reminds you of the grounds around the clubhouse at Augusta National.

"When I've really got it going good, I do this," Elkington says, dropping a golf ball onto a tightly mowed strip of grass next to his driveway. He pulls a two iron from his black and white golf bag. "No, Steve, don't!" you want to say as he takes his stance, in the tone you'd use to implore someone not to jump off a ledge.

The target is invisible, a (hopefully) empty paddock, hidden away two hundred or so yards in the distance. Elkington's shot will have to rise like a rocket to clear, in order, the family car—a forest-green Chevy Suburban parked just twelve steps away—a towering privet hedge, and a grove of tall pecan trees shading the unsuspecting horses. The ball must also pierce a narrow piece of sky framed left and right by his own and his neighbor's expensive houses and their expensive windows.

Stephen John Elkington swings. Both the rhythmic ease of his stroke and the danger of the shot cause you to suck in your breath, but the ball sizzles over the car, over the hedge, past the windows, and through the swaying peaks of the fifty-foot-tall trees.

"No divot, see," Elkington says casually, then he drops another ball and hits the shot again, with the same result. "Sometimes I'll hit it out there with a driver, from this little crack in the concrete," he says. "But I move the car for that one."

Such surreal takeoffs and landings are vintage Elkington. During a long rain delay at the Shark Shootout in 1997, he looked out his window and spotted a pleasing target on the deserted golf course. Hmmm . . . He opened the glass patio doors of his course-side condominium, checked the ceiling height to see if there was room to swing, then moved a couch and chairs and lamps and two guests this way and that. "About 145. Seven iron, I think," he mused aloud. "Better start it low."

Drivers from the driveway and irons off the carpet and out the door are symptoms of both Elkington's attitude toward and obsession with the game. He is, in short, a golf nut, a man who tees it up against the bandits at nearby Champions Golf Club on his days off and settles his bets afterward over a beer. He collects (and reads) golf books, and his knowledge of the game and its players is encyclopedic. A USGA official says Elkington knows the rules of golf better than any player he's ever met. A diarist, he regularly records his thoughts on golf and life in a notebook in his meticulously neat office. He works out like a fiend, every day. He's the primary spokesman for the conservation group Audubon International. He knows the common and the Latin names for each of the 150 species of plants, trees, and shrubs he's planted around his house, and he weeds his elaborate garden himself. He hates soft spikes.

In fact, Elkington is a fierce traditionalist in everything related to golf, which, ironically, makes him something of an iconoclast. He says, for example, "Most of today's golf clubs are the worst ever made." And: "Golf instruction today has no meat, no overriding theme. It's all faults-and-fixes, which is absolute rubbish." And: "The influx of new players to golf is a real problem, because so many of them have no education about golf."

Perhaps most revealingly, Elkington's two closest advisers (don't use the word "guru" around him, or them) are wise old golf pros, both of them more than twice his age: Alex Mercer of Sydney, Australia, and Jack Burke, Jr., known as Jackie, the owner-operator of Champions Golf Club in Houston.

New South Wales Golf Club, near Sydney, Australia. Alex Mercer and his most successful student, the day after Elkington lived a dream for both men by winning the 1992 Australian Open. "We may have had a few beers that afternoon," recalls Elkington.

The relationship with Mercer began in 1976. When as teenagers Steve and his older brother, Rob, were named to the New South Wales junior boys team, one of their rewards was regular lessons with Mercer, the pro at Royal Sydney Golf Club and the most respected teacher in Australia. He'd been a hell of a player in his day, too, winning twenty-three important tournaments. And he would have won more, if not for his great rival, five-time British Open champion Peter Thomson. "Alex Mercer wouldn't even see you if your hair wasn't combed or if your clothes were wrinkled," Elkington recalls. "And if your shoes weren't shined, your clubs clean, and your face shaved, you could forget about getting any of his time." Steve and Rob would take the Friday midnight train from their home in Wagga Wagga, a dusty, inland town on the other side of the Great Dividing Mountain range. They'd shine their shoes, clean their clubs, and play cards and talk all night. Eight hours later, the train would chug into the station in Sydney. Alex Mercer would be there waiting.

"Steve and I decided early on we would not be after a 'correct' swing but an efficient swing," says Mercer, a friendly but direct man, and still Elkington's teacher. "It really gets up my nose when people talk about his 'natural' swing. He's worked extremely hard to get it. His work ethic is absolutely insatiable.

"Steve began with no bad habits, and developed his game without paying any attention to fads. I'm awfully suspicious of instruction from someone who came to the game with some severe problem, like a big looping hook. His swing will be a correction of his worst mistakes. Not a swing to learn from."

Burke, the 1956 Masters and PGA champion, has gradually assumed the role of Elkington's metaphysical guide since their first meeting in 1982. Elkington was then an eighteen-year-old freshman at the University of Houston, a wiry, somewhat wild young man with a restless mind and an IQ of 140. He assuaged his intellect and his inevitable homesickness by immersing himself deeper and deeper in golf. And he gravitated to the garrulous, magnificently opinionated Burke, just as he had to Mercer.

"A lot of the University of Houston kids have visited us at Champions, a lot of great players," says Burke, maintaining impossible-to-break eye contact. "But the thing that always interested me about Steve was that he was willing to change. Most kids think they've got it. Steve never thought that. He

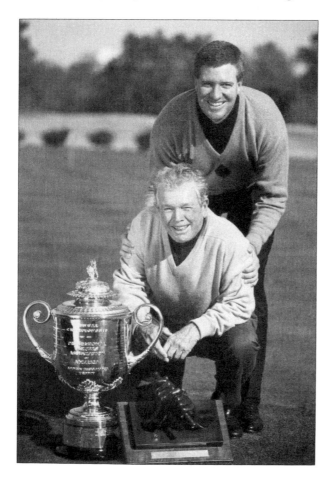

Elkington and Burke pose with trophies they both have won, the Vardon (for low stroke average on the Tour) and the Wannamaker (for the PGA Championship). "I couldn't have won either without Jackie's help," says Elkington.

knew that this is a game of adjustments with a stick and a ball.

"But I don't teach people what to do. I just enjoy talking golf. I like the stories of the game, and you can learn from that. Steve likes the golf environment, and he stays around people who like it. And he's a good guy to have around, because he's a good storyteller himself. And very bright."

Years later, Burke would look out his window at seven A.M. and often see Elkington sitting on his porch, reading the newspaper. Waiting for the old pro to invite him in for a cup of coffee and a talk.

"I'm not his guru, his father, his manager, or his mentor. I'm no crutch he uses," the ex-marine concludes. "Elkie's his own man."

For years now—at least since 1995, when he won the PGA Championship and the Vardon Trophy for the lowest stroke average on the PGA Tour—everyone's been asking Steve Elkington the same question: How do you hit the ball so far, with so much control, yet with so little effort?

The implication that he averaged 69.62 strokes for an entire year and won a major (tying the lowest score ever shot in one of golf's big four tournaments) without trying irks Elk a little bit. So does the corollary comment that his swing of beauty was a genetic gift, like curly hair. Deflecting the familiar questions with ease, he assures the curious that his stroke is not merely a lucky inheritance from Ross and Margaret Elkington, and that he *is* trying, by God. How he got his elegantly simple swing is a bit complicated, Elkington says.

It doesn't *look* complicated. People watch him on the course or on the practice tee, and wonder: Could I do that? Elkington's golf swing is both an amazing visual treat for amateur observers and the envy of his peers, linking in its power and grace a ballerina's feathery *tour en l'air* and a railroad worker driving steel spikes. "Elkington has the best swing out there," says Sam Snead, who had the move everyone aspired to in an earlier era. "Great rhythm, great balance, great follow-through. He's wonderful to watch." There's no question what most of the other pros think: For four years in a row, a jury of his peers has voted his swing the best on the Tour.

Everyone tells him he should write a book.

He's taken his time. Through reading, discussion, observation, and his own experiments, the owner of the best swing in golf has now distilled his thoughts down to a handful of essential truths. "I don't believe in quick fixes, which is what most written teaching promises," Elkington says. "I believe in fundamentals. You have to learn to play golf, just as you have to learn to read or to type or to play the piano. A proper grip, setup, and swing are not instinctive. The game should be learned from ground zero.

"In no way do I think the fundamentals of the game are easy. On the contrary. But I believe I can give the reader a distinct method to understand, and then to learn, the basics. The goal is a book that will stand the test of time, not a how-to cure of today's problem."

Of the one hundred or so instruction books in his library, Elkington returns again and again to only two, both of them golden oldies: *Five Lessons* by Ben Hogan (first published in 1957) and *Sam Snead on Golf* (1961) by Sam Snead. The old masters have the most credence with Elkington; he's found that middling practitioners tend to make an academic exercise out of golf, focusing on the frozen images from a high-speed camera and claiming great insight from the dissection. "The swing is a continuous flow of movement, and we destroy its continuous character if we divide it arbitrarily," Percy Boomer wrote in *On Learning Golf* in 1942. Elkington agrees.

Another, somewhat ironic problem Elkington has with modern instruction is its preoccupation with the swing. Although many have said that Elkington makes the prettiest stroke since Snead, low score wins in golf, not best aesthetics. Elkington wins some of the biggest and best tournaments because he's one of the best bunker players in the world, because he rarely misses a four-footer, and because in the midst of the most terrifying pressure, he makes everything he looks at. Witness his final-round 64 at the 1995 PGA; and the twenty-footer he made on the play-off hole; and the string of eleventh-hour birdies he made in winning Greensboro in 1990 and The Players Championship in 1991 (featuring a three iron from a divot on the final hole, and a fifteen-foot putt); and the thirty-footers he made to win the Tournament of Champions in play-offs in 1992 and 1996.

"His strength is that he's one of the few guys who play golf *as a game*," says Burke. "He works the ball. He's got imagination, and adaptability."

"His mind is his greatest strength," says Mercer. Obviously, Steve Elkington has more to offer than just the purity of his full shots.

He decided to write this book now partly because he's hit on a way to escape the trap of static photography. Elkington here reintroduces an idea not much seen for half a century: the flicker, or flip, book. By lifting the corners or edges of this book with the thumb and allowing the pages to fall in sequence, the reader will—it is hoped—be reminded that a golf swing is a motion, not a series of poses, and of the power of rhythm. A comment from Alex Mercer is on point: "I never gave a lesson to Steve—or to anyone—without talking about rhythm and tempo."

Elkington avoids the faults-and-fixes pandemic quite simply, by—for the most part—not discussing them.

And because many readers of this book will be highly golf-literate and well informed, Elkington has dedicated a section at the end of each chapter to the advanced student. For example, at the end of Chapter 3, Elkington reveals a simple move to add as much as twenty yards to the tee shot.

A final difference between this and most other instruction books is that this one has a little more biography in it, because the story of how Steve Elkington developed his smooth and powerful golf swing can be told only through the story of his life. "If you know a bit about what I've done to swing like I do, and why," Elkington says, "that will help you build your own swing."

FIVE FUNDAMENTALS

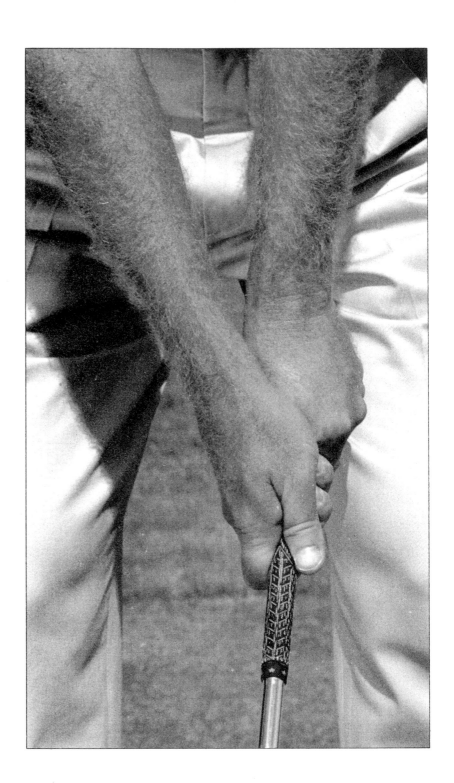

1

THE GRIP

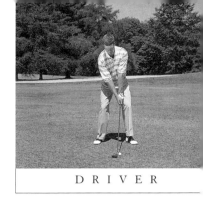

DRIVER

AFTER ALEX MERCER collected the Elkington brothers at the train station, often as not he would take them to practice and play at New South Wales Golf Club. The course occupies a dramatic plateau in a national park in south Sydney overlooking rockbound Botany Bay, where Captain James Cook landed when he discovered Australia in 1770. Another Englishman, golf architect Alister Mackenzie, came to this exact spot 150 years later; Mackenzie, who would gain renown for designing Cypress Point, Augusta National, and Royal Melbourne, also laid out the holes at New South Wales Golf Club.

"You always hear about Mackenzie's other courses, but in my opinion this is the best golf course in the world," Elkington says. "*This* is golf in the kingdom. Just watch." He walks up the wide fifth fairway, which becomes so steep that all that is visible for a few moments is the grass in front and the sky above. We reach the crest of the hill, and stop, and suddenly a stunning vista of rolling ground and waves crashing on rocks reveals itself.

DRIVER

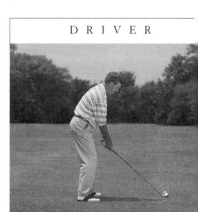

"Julie Andrews, *The Sound of Music*," someone says. " 'The hills are alive . . .' "

"Nah," says Elkington. "Something with helicopters, and machine guns, and Sylvester Stallone hanging off a rope."

"Steve was about thirteen when he came to me," recalls Mercer. "Yes, you could see even then that he wanted to be great. I've seen heaps of people who'd like to be the best, but if you show them how much hard work is involved, it doesn't take them long to drop. Hard work never daunted Steve. . . . Eight hours on a train. How keen can you get? Then he and Rob would get back on the train on Sunday afternoon and make it to school on Monday.

Bonnie Dune Golf Club, Sydney, about 1978. The coltish Elkington shows good extension as he rips one off the first tee in a state tournament.

The Grip

"His swing was not the same as it is now. He was very lanky, and like all young teenagers built like that he was a little flippy-wristed at the top of the backswing. He had a little more lateral slide, and his swing was upright, too upright. But he already had a little flair about him, and a real determination to make a score at the end of a hole. He just looked at that golf course, and at the other players, and thought, Well, whatever they can do, I can do the same or better.

"I've been researching the game since the days of Harry Vardon, and I've discovered that the basics have remained the same since the days of hickory shafts: grip, posture, balance, alignment, and feel.

"Unless you're absolutely sure of these basic parts of your technique, you won't be able to let your rhythm and timing take over."

DRIVER

DRIVER

7

I CAN TAKE a guy off the street, put a club in his hand, and in five minutes make him set up to the ball like me. Like someone you wouldn't want to bet.

That's because the three most important things in golf require little movement and no talent whatsoever. They are grip, stance, and posture. Learning them correctly requires some discipline and practice, but they don't take from your supply of talent.

I've always thought of a person's native talent as a glass, filled with ability in liquid form. I'm fascinated that these three key components of the swing can be learned without spilling or drinking a drop. But the further you get from a fundamentally sound grip, stance, and posture, the more you'll have to drain from the glass. Obviously, you'd be better off saving that talent for hitting the ball.

I admit to being almost obsessed with the grip. Soon after I took up golf, I used to walk the three miles to school with a twelve-inch piece of a club, just a grip on a cut-off shaft. And I'd pull that grip out of my backpack just to practice holding on to it. Alex Mercer had given me an intriguing thought: that I could have the best grip of anyone in the world, better even than Jack Nicklaus's.

In time, hands powerfully but thoughtfully formed on a club began to appeal to me on both an artistic and a professional level. I have a bronze of Harry Vardon's grip (the 1995 Vardon Trophy) in a glass case behind my desk, and I look at it often. It's a wonderful reminder of where it all started.

I remember watching Ben Crenshaw give a clinic in Austin, Texas, in which he never got past how you put your hands on a club. Two hours, and that's all he talked about. He got so

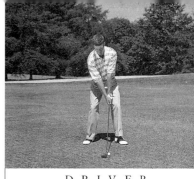

DRIVER

into it he forgot to hit any balls. Probably most of the people there were absolutely aghast, not believing that they were listening to all this about only one part of the golf game. But I thought it was the most interesting talk I'd ever heard about golf technique.

The best grippers—Crenshaw, Nick Faldo, Jack Burke, and my coach, Alex Mercer, for example—give the impression that the club is a toothpick in their hands. People tell me that the club looks very small in my hands, too. That doesn't necessarily relate to the size of the hands; in fact, I have relatively short fingers, and wear only a medium-large-size glove. No, the illusion of a tiny stick in giant mitts given by a good grip is a result of the hands dominating the club.

When Ben Crenshaw isn't playing well, all he talks about is his grip. I'm the same way. I've never played poorly when my grip felt great.

The grip connects to every part of the game. For example: Everyone remarks that I never dawdle or waste time over a shot. Alex Mercer's explanation for this is that because I hold the club so well, I don't have any conflicting thoughts in my mind. When no confusion clouds your thoughts, when you're absolutely comfortable holding the club, you can play with ease. What's at work here is centering, a concept from Zen philosophy. The centered person is at peace. Just as a child may be uneasy without his favorite toy, or a violinist may feel anxious until he holds his instrument, I don't feel calmness and capability flow into me until I pick up one of my clubs.

My grip, in other words, is a key to my swing. I'll talk more about this in the chapter on the swing and swing tempo. For now I'll just say that the further you are from a correct, comfortable grip, the further you are from being a good or a better golfer.

DRIVER

...

FROM THIS POINT on, remember that all the things you read here are equally important. The linking of the fundamentals is the key.

I do not profess that the basics of golf are easy. In fact, some are quite difficult. But the great thing about golf is that you get out of it what you put into it.

Please note: All the instruction in this book assumes the reader is right-handed.

THE FOREFINGER

Before you even pick up the club, consider the forefinger (also known as the first finger or the index finger).

Be prepared to essentially glue this digit to the sides of its next-door neighbor, the thumb. Do this on both hands. When I was a kid and just learning the game, Alex Mercer had me walk around for a week with my thumbs never leaving the sides of the forefingers. I'd even pick coins out of my pockets with my thumbs and forefingers fused together. This fusion helps my hands encircle the club so completely that you cannot stick your finger into any part of my grip and pry open my fingers. If I had to have an operation to help my golf, I'd have the doctor sew my forefingers to my thumbs.

I emphasize this connection for two reasons. First, by not allowing any holes or gaps in your grip—no leakages, as I like to put it—your grip will not slip. Second, it gives your hands a feeling of wholeness, or togetherness, so the hands never feel as if they're at cross-purposes.

The Grip

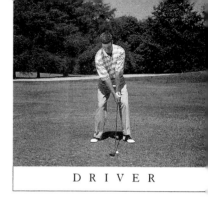

DRIVER

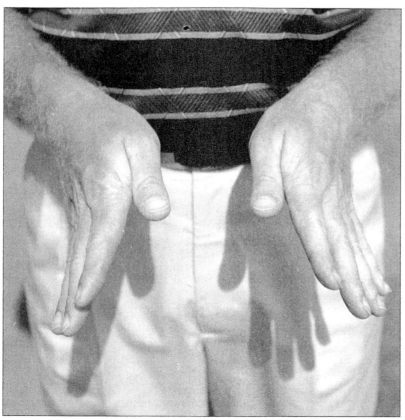

Glue your thumb and forefinger together on both hands to keep your grip from slipping and to make your hands work as a unit.

DRIVER

11

THE LEFT HAND

It is not difficult to get the left hand on the grip in the proper way. Let's start by surveying a small part of the hand's anatomy. Hold your left hand up, palm toward you, then fold your fingers in slightly. Notice the several deep wrinkles in that palm. The deepest and topmost line is called the *distal palmar crease* (distal means farthest from the center). The club lies above that wrinkle, along the base of the fingers. The left-hand grip is not in the palm, but not entirely in the fingers; but if you were to err, it should be on the side of the fingers.

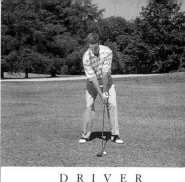

DRIVER

Now, with the thumb connected to the forefinger, close the left hand around the handle. The thumb falls wherever it may, most likely on the center of the grip.

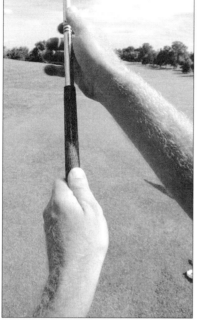
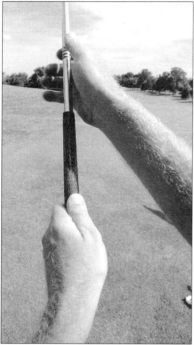

Its exact location will be determined by the size and conformation of the hand. Keep the thumb on top of the club as much as possible, and make sure the line formed by the thumb and forefinger is pointed at the right shoulder.

Strong or weak? I can hear you ask, and How many knuckles should I be able to see? In most golf instruction there is a lot of emphasis on whether the left hand should be turned to the right, so its back is facing the sky (a "strong" grip), or turned to the left, toward the target (a "weak" grip). I don't get into that, because if you've done both the two simple steps in left-hand gripping I've talked about, your grip will be neither too strong nor too weak.

DRIVER

Put it this way: You should be able to look down as you address the ball and see two knuckles of the left hand. That's very orthodox instruction, and I agree with it. The two-knuckle grip is neither strong nor weak, but neutral.

A final point about the left hand: The heel of your hand should never overlap the end of the club. In other words, the butt of the club should be entirely underneath the pad of the hand, so the entire hand is flush on the handle. Allowing part of your hand to hang off the grip will diminish your power, and your control of the club.

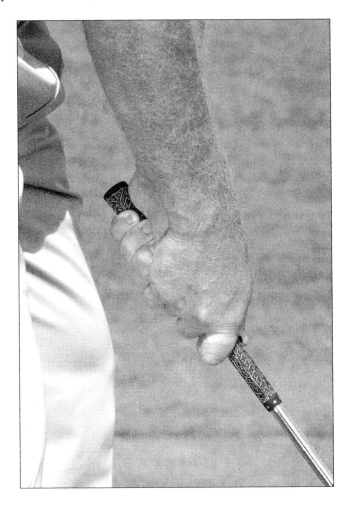

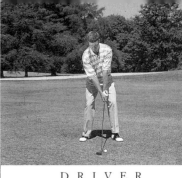

THE RIGHT HAND

Most instructors have it that for the right-handed player the left hand is the more important, but I disagree strongly. The right hand is twice as important as the left, and ten times trickier to get on the club correctly. More important because the right hand dictates the right-arm position and how the club will set at the top of the backswing, where everything can go completely wrong—or exactly right. Trickier because a golf club is thinner than anything else we hold to hit a ball; it's much thinner than a tennis racket, for instance, or a cricket or baseball bat. For most people, a correct right-hand grip definitely feels unnatural.

But the right hand, wrist, and arm are crucial in golf. I believe it's no coincidence that virtually all the amputee golf champions are right-armed, not left-armed.

Think fingertips for your right-hand grip. If a drink with a straw was on the table in front of you, you'd instinctively draw the straw to your lips with your fingertips. Painters and calligraphers naturally hold their brushes in the fingertips, so they have freedom and flow in their wrists. But another instinct too often causes golfers to grip a golf club too much in the palm, presumably because a golf club is a heavier, less delicate object than a straw or a brush. But a golf club needs to be held more sensitively and precisely than does a baseball bat.

Again, begin by holding up your right hand, palm side facing you. You'll notice the two deep grooves that separate the three sections of each of the fingers. These are called the *inter-phalangeal creases*, and they provide a map for the placement of the club in the right hand. The club lies right in the center of the approximately one-inch-wide center section of the

15

fingers. The tips of the fingers—*distal pads* is the anatomical term—curl around to hold the club.

The pinkie finger fits on top of the forefinger of the left hand, with absolutely no pressure or grab. The important gripping fingers are at the bottom of your right hand, the thumb and forefinger. I believe you should practice occasionally with the pinkie finger off the club.

The top of the left thumb should be secured against the lifeline of the right palm.

The Grip

The right thumb's contact with the club is tiny, but surpassingly important. Alex Mercer used to take a marker and draw a little spot on the right side of the pad of my right thumb. That spot is the right thumb's only point of contact with the grip.

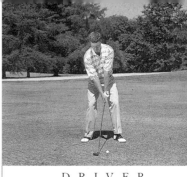

DRIVER

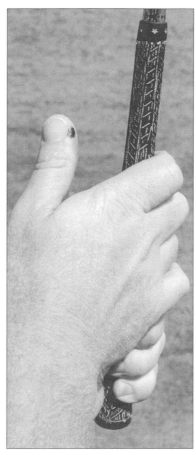

Just as with the left-hand grip, the line formed by the thumb and forefinger should point to the right shoulder. This union at the bottom of your grip forms what I call the saddle. A properly formed saddle is the only way to make the club face stay square on its journey throughout the swing. (See photo, page 18.)

(See photo, page 18.)

DRIVER

17

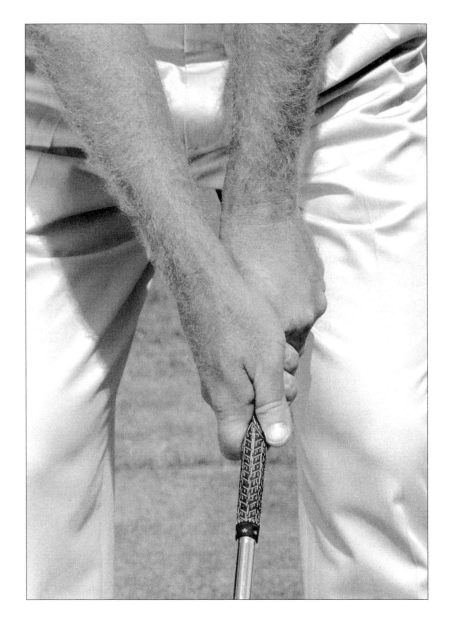

As for the length of my grip—how much of the club is covered by my hands—I think all the fingers should have their place on the grip. The hands should neither be mashed together nor spread out, but comfortable and secure, dominating the club.

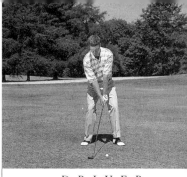

DRIVER

SOME FINAL THOUGHTS ON THE GRIP

Like most serious golfers, I prefer the Vardon grip, in which the little finger of the right hand overlaps on top of the index finger of the left hand.

A few good players—Jack Nicklaus among them—use the interlocking grip (though Jack hardly interlocks at all). In this method, the little finger of the right hand goes inside that same space in the left-hand fingers and forms a pincer with the left index finger. Some people with small hands feel this gives them a little extra holding power.

But beware of interlocking too tightly. That's where power *isn't*. A tight grip is usually too deep into the palm of the right hand, not in the fingers, where it belongs.

A third method, the ten-finger or baseball grip, adds more wrist to your swing, and that's fine. But if that's the grip that's most comfortable to you, you have to understand its effect on your swing. You'll become a hands player and inevitably a less smooth swinger than you will if you use a Vardon grip. And less smoothness inevitably means less consistent striking. Art Wall, the 1959 Masters champion, used the ten-finger grip. He may have been the exception that proves the rule.

A lot is made of grip pressure, but I believe that if you hold the club correctly this part of the grip equation will take care of itself. Undoubtedly, there's a lot of excessive grip pressure in the land, but this is nearly always the result of an instinctive feeling that the club could slip because of a faulty grip.

"Oh hell, the club slipped," someone will say after a bad shot in a pressure situation. I remember Claude Harmon's reply to this time-worn excuse: "Did the club slip—or was it

DRIVER

DRIVER

your heart?" In other words, a lack of confidence in your grip can and does cause nervous swings.

How tightly should you hold the club? Tight. Perhaps "very secure" is a better description. I don't think you can grip the club too hard if you grip it correctly. Not that I have a death grip on it, but I have the feeling that three guys couldn't pull the club out of my hands. Everything is clamped down and sealed off. And I have the pressure in the right spots.

Possibly the foregoing will tempt you to change your grip. Well, if it needs to be done, have no fear, just do it. Often you'll hear teachers say, "Well, this change will make you play lousy for two months, and then you'll start to play better." I've never believed in that. I've always felt that if you make a change that really needs to be made, then you will improve immediately.

DRIVER

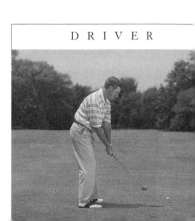

FOR THE ADVANCED PLAYER

As you know, there are two types of grips, round and ribbed. Ribbed grips, which I use, have an oval cross section, with a thickened line through the bottom of the grip at six o'clock. With ribbed grips, I feel I have a reference point for soling the club squarely each time, and a distinct spot for my hands, which I don't get with round grips.

My specifications: Victory Cord grips, size 60, ribbed, with one spiral wrap of three-quarter-inch tape underneath. Size 58 is a standard industry size for men; size 60 is a little smaller, and 62 is smaller still, for women, children, or men with small hands. (Diameter is, of course, also affected by the use of tape beneath the grip.)

The correct grip size is as important as the right shoe size. But a proper fit is not only a matter of how big your hands are. Most club fitters will merely measure your hands and select a grip for you, but an equally important consideration is how you hold the club. If you hold the club as I've recommended— primarily in the fingers—you may well need a thinner grip. Fat grips tend to make you hold the club in your palms.

In the summer, when sweat can make a club a bit harder to hold on to, I use grips with more cord. In the winter, I go to a soft rubber grip. I go thinner when I play in England late in the year, because a smaller grip helps the feel. I also consider a thinner grip when hot weather makes the hands puff up.

Each of my grips must weigh 50 grams. Few club makers bother to check this, even though grips from the same box can vary by as much as 8 grams. This could make the swing weight—the ratio of the head weight to the grip end—vary by

The Grip

a full point, even two. A golf club is supposed to be a balanced instrument, so why not have a balanced set of grips?

Although many people think it's just decoration, the pattern embossed on the grip I use has an important practical use. It's called a grip guide. It provides a road map for the placement of the thumbs and shows how far down the club your grip should extend. I never fail to use it.

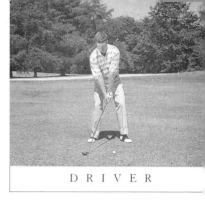

D R I V E R

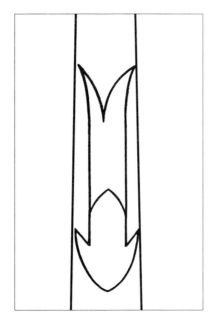

All Victory Grips feature this design.

D R I V E R

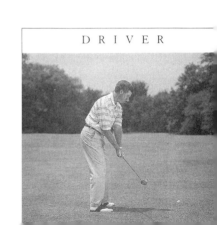

DRIVER

A GRIPPING TALE

When I traveled to Scotland in 1979 to represent Australia in the Junior World Cup, I went into a butcher shop in St. Andrews to buy some sausages; our team was staying in a dormitory at the university, and we cooked our own meals. The butcher asked me what I was in town for besides sausages, and when I told him he reached behind him for a golf club. "Let's see your grip, lad," he said. I'll never forget that moment: There I was in the home of golf, and a stranger in a bloody apron wants to talk with me about the golf grip. So I held the club for him, and he said he was going to look in the bookmakers' shop for my name and the odds on me and my team. By my grip alone, he was game to put a wager on me. Then I asked the butcher to show me his grip. He had huge hands, but he put them on the club as delicately and precisely as a surgeon. When he told me he was a quite competent player—a seven handicap on the Old Course, and a five on the New—it didn't surprise me at all.

In some golf cultures—the United States in particular—it's common for someone to ask you to take your club to the top of the backswing and hold it. But in Australia and in Scotland, the focus is on the grip, anything to do with the grip, including how big your grips are and what they are made of.

DRIVER

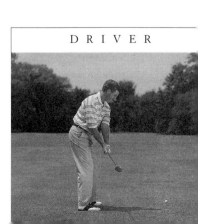

DRIVER

Ben Crenshaw, Jack Burke, and Elkington share a laugh during a late-season round at Champions Golf Club, Houston. Elkington loves social golf.

DRIVER

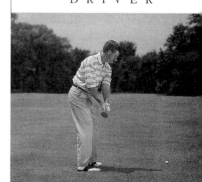

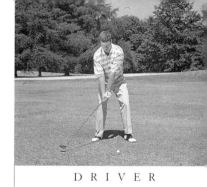

2

THE SETUP

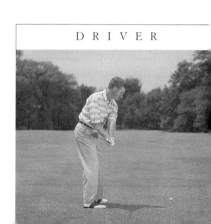

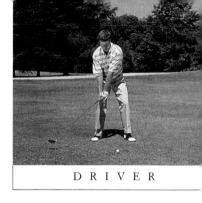

DRIVER

THE ELKINGTON FAMILY lived on the Australian bush bank managers circuit, moving from Penrith to Narrabri to Goulburn to Wagga Wagga and to Wollongong. Ross Elkington's employers lent the money for farmers to plant their crops and to build their barns and homes; Rob and Steve went to school, held odd jobs, and played games. Steve worked a paper route, wielded a cleaver in a slaughterhouse, and, inevitably, worked as a caddie, greens mower, and shop assistant at a golf course. Before golf took thorough possession of his son's leisure time, Ross remembers that little Steve was exceedingly adept with a soccer ball and a cricket bat. He played mid-on or silly mid-on on the cricket pitch; the baseball equivalent is third base, playing in for a bunt.

At age seventeen, Steve won the Australasian Amateur; at eighteen, he won the Doug Sanders World Junior. At this point a curious Saturday-morning ritual developed. The phone would ring at six A.M. and on the line would be an American with a soft voice and an evangelist's style. "Hi, Elkie, Coach Williams," the man would say. "You still hittin' it great? Real

DRIVER

31

good, real good. You know, we're gonna have a great team next year, even though we lost Freddie Couples. Yeah, he turned pro. But we can build a real good team with you and Billy Ray Brown, real good, real good. Yes, we'd love to have you. Okay, Elkie, we'll talk to you again soon." (Dave Williams, the coach of a record sixteen NCAA championship teams, had introduced himself at the World Junior in Houston.) After months of this, Elkington stopped the transglobal wake-up calls the only way he could, by accepting a golf scholarship to the University of Houston—to the dismay of the folks at the University of Sydney (among others), who had offered him an art scholarship.

Elkington employed an expert caddie in the '96 Masters in his older brother, Robert. A Titleist golf equipment salesman and the father of four, Robert Elkington is one of the best amateur golfers in Australia.

The Setup

"When I went to America, it shocked a lot of people," Elkington recalls. "Some viewed me as a traitor." The nation's press bemoaned his departure, with headlines like GOLFER IN EXILE. "For my mother, my leaving was like her child had gone off to war," says Elkington. "Not that I took it too well myself. I was homesick constantly." As everyone in the family understood, Steve would not be flying home on weekends to do his laundry; the seventeen-hour Houston–Los Angeles–Sydney flight cost about $3,000—no trifle on a bush bank manager's salary. In fact, during his four years at the University of Houston, he returned to Australia just twice.

This led to several Dickensian scenes. There were the winter weekends when seemingly everyone had left the campus—except for two solitary figures, Elkington hitting practice balls on a field near Hofheinz Pavilion and a lithe, muscular young man running miles on a nearby track. Eventually, they introduced themselves: "Hi, Steve Elkington." "Hi, Clyde Drexler." Drexler would later star for Portland and Houston in the National Basketball Association.

One night during Christmas vacation, the loneliest few weeks for the expatriated Australian, Elkington returned from dinner to his empty dormitory, the metallic click of the closing door echoing behind him. He turned a corner and suddenly beheld an almost seven-foot-tall black man coming from the opposite direction. Both froze for a moment. "Hi, I'm Steve Elkington." "Hello, Hakeem Olajuwon." Olajuwon, Drexler's basketball teammate from Nigeria, would also develop into one of the best players in college and professional basketball.

The fax machine became Elkington's lifeline to home and hearth and to Alex Mercer. "One part of my reply to his swing questions or problems has always been the same," Mercer says.

DRIVER

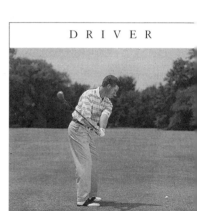

DRIVER

" 'Trust your swing,' I'll write in the fax, and underline it about six times."

"When he went off to college was when he really got good," observes Elkington's brother Rob. Steve had beaten his older brother before, most memorably with a hole in one with a three iron on the final hole of the Wagga Wagga Country Club championship. But he'd never beaten Mercer. In the summer of '82, at Royal Sydney Golf Club, it finally happened. And it was hard to tell if the student or the teacher was happier about it.

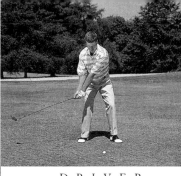

DRIVER

ALEX MERCER TOLD me once that I'd spend half my time as a golfer learning the fundamentals of the game, and the other half of my time forgetting them.

He meant that after you've ingrained the basics, you need not continually relearn them. The basics should not remain entirely buried in the subconscious mind, however. I run through a little checklist before I hit a shot. It takes only a second or two, because practice and repetition have created a feeling of what is correct.

Most golfers are in turmoil over what mechanical thing to think about as they prepare to hit a shot. Head down, left arm straight, and so on. It seems the modern pre-shot prescription to break this mental gridlock goes something like this: You get behind the ball, take a few deep breaths, visualize a good shot, and walk in with a positive frame of mind. But I've never in my life seen a great player use this procedure, and it doesn't seem to solve the basic question of aim.

A great player prepares to hit this way: He finds his target; selects his shot and picks a club to accomplish it; gets the club out and gets his grip established; then walks into address, always in motion. It's a dance step.

And what is the accomplished player thinking about as he prepares to hit? *His one and only focus is the target:* a side of the fairway, a specific part of the green, the flagstick, the bridge on the fifth hole, or the hillock on the fourteenth. Not deep breaths, not positive thinking; his visual and mental concentration on the target blocks out all else and begins the instant he chooses what to aim for. Having mastered the grip and his aim, his mind is free to think of golf's real goal, the target— which frees his body to make good golf swings.

DRIVER

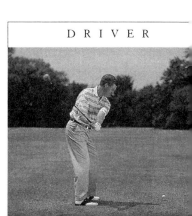

In short, the more conscious you are of aiming, the better you hit the ball. I know some pretty crafty golfers who play a somewhat homely fade on every shot. They may not have much versatility, but because they know how to aim, they're hard to beat.

Many handicap players expend too much effort visualizing the shot. But unless you know and can put in place the setup and swing that will make the desired result happen, visualization is a fairy tale. My goal is to get you organized into such a good platform that very little psychologizing will be required. You'll swing with great freedom and a certain serenity every time.

This most vital part of the golf swing should not be a great drain on your ability. Like the grip, the interrelated fundamentals of aim, alignment, and posture are basic skills that take only a small amount from your glass of talent.

Although they may seem static, aim, alignment, and posture actually require a good bit of movement. I'm in motion from the moment I take the club from my caddie until I finish my follow-through. You can't just stand there!

Let's go through this step by step, and you'll see how aim, posture, and alignment connect like the skin on an apple.

You need not duplicate my routine to the letter, but it wouldn't harm you if you did. My pre-shot procedure, like my swing, was built to be devoid of quirks. There's nothing in it that's not well thought out and built to last.

And please bear in mind that while the following may seem like a lot of detail, I actually play quite quickly. I recommend that you do, too. Generally speaking, every shot should present a decision between only two clubs, a five iron or a six, or a three iron and a four wood, for example. So select a club, and don't attempt to untangle your emotions or sort out your problems as you prepare to hit. Just pick a target, make a decision, and get on with it!

I take my grip, left hand first, and put it up in front of me. I look to make sure I've put my left hand on the club correctly before I put my right hand on it. Don't take this step for granted. I've been playing golf almost all my life, and I still give my grip a little visual check before each swing.

I find my target while standing behind the ball, and I think deeply about the target while I walk to the ball. Conversation stops. After all, you're on the golf course for a reason, and

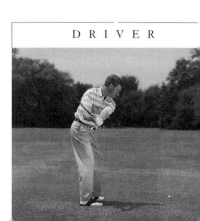

DRIVER

This is the time to make the target as small as possible.

DRIVER

37

that's to play golf. Idle chats with opponents or friends have their place, but I enjoy thinking golf.

The target should be as small and specific as possible; without a precise aiming point, you can lose focus to a mechanical thought or to a worry about the result. If you don't aim at anything, you'll hit it every time.

Sport psychologist Bob Rotella once posed this question: What part of a blank dartboard would you aim at? If you painted a bull's-eye in the center of the board, there's no doubt you'd aim for that. The moral is: Find bull's-eyes for every shot, and aim for them every time.

Familiarity definitely helps in aiming. You usually play better at your home course, because familiar targets create a bigger, more complete picture of the job at hand. Eventually, you want to get so competent at selecting targets and aiming at them that this crucial step is almost automatic.

My feeling at this moment, my attitude, is of being capable. Not confident, which implies a certain ebb and flow; everyone's confidence goes up and down. My sense of being absolutely prepared, aware, and competent for the matter at hand is the best feeling in the world.

I put my right hand on. You should take your grip before you place the club behind the ball. If you settle your grip after you've taken your stance, you'll lose your focus on the target, and probably line up incorrectly.

While still standing behind the ball, **I take a little half-swing,** my eyes on the target. I make sure I scuff the ground when I do this; like a baseball or cricket player pounding his bat before the ball arrives, or a basketball player bouncing the ball a few times before shooting a free throw, I'm orienting myself to Mother Earth.

The Setup

I occasionally think of the club as a rifle at this point, aimed dead at my target, and with my feet parallel to the line to the target.

While a swing thought at this stage is entirely appropriate, don't clutter your mind by getting into these big, full practice swings. The effort to make a perfect practice swing simply isn't worth it; even if you make a perfect practice swing, what have you got? And how many times have you hit a bad shot simply because you couldn't get the right feel in your rehearsal?

Furthermore, Ben Hogan once told me that practice swings are a waste of time and energy. I haven't taken another one since!

I approach the ball obliquely, my eyes still burning into the target, **with my right shoulder quite obviously dropped several**

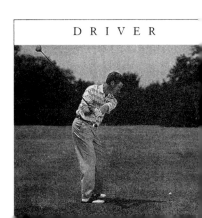

DRIVER

Think, look, and feel the shot.

inches lower than my left. The tilted walk to the ball has two purposes: First, since the right hand is below the left on the grip, the right shoulder has to be lower. Second, this posture pre-sets the impact position, in which the left shoulder is up.

This procedure is so simple and so important, yet so seldom followed by most golfers. If you wish to improve, you must make it a part of your routine.

I consider this posture to be important enough that I sometimes find myself unconsciously practicing it while standing at home, or in the locker room, or while waiting for a plane. I must look as though I have a stitch in my side.

Three things happen simultaneously when I get to the ball: **I swivel my head from the target back to the ball;**

The Setup

I sole my club behind the ball square to the line I've chosen; and I step up a little too close to the ball with my right foot.

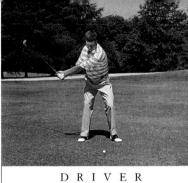

DRIVER

DRIVER

41

The right foot placement is experimental at this point; in a few seconds I'll set my left foot, then adjust the right so that I have the ball position and distance from the ball I want. You always want to come in a little too close, then back off, because we all know once you stand too far away you never move back in; it just doesn't seem to be human nature. But the main point is that you must commit your club to the line before you commit your feet.

I've never had any success at aiming at a piece of grass or whatever just in front of the ball. I prefer to look out at the actual target.

I set the left foot,

Notice that my eyes are still involved with the target; the club has not yet been soled.

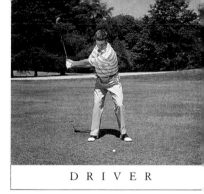

DRIVER

then adjust my right foot. When I met Ken Venturi for the first time, he told me I must be a good golfer because I walk like a duck! And in fact I've always felt that the golfer's feet should be like a duck's, splayed out at ten minutes to two o'clock. Left foot at the ten, right foot at the two. Ten minutes to two allows your hips their full range of motion.

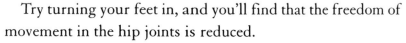

Try turning your feet in, and you'll find that the freedom of movement in the hip joints is reduced.

As you might expect, I vary the width of my stance all the time. My feet are at their greatest distance apart, with the inside of my insteps directly under my shoulders, when I hit a driver. I take a smaller stance with the shorter clubs.

I have never believed there is one ball position in golf. In fact, given all the game's variables, I don't know if any two are ever exactly the same! Rarely are two lies or two situations identical; you get to hit a particular shot in golf only once. Ball

DRIVER

placement calls for an ability to adapt and is an opportunity to be creative, which is the greatest part of our game.

For example, a seven iron shot over water might make you want to put the ball back in your stance a little, to ensure clean contact. The ball may fly lower, but it will probably be dry. In the opposite case, when you want a high shot out of rough or to clear a tree, you'll play the ball way forward, even opposite the left toe.

Most of the time, my stance is slightly open. That is, my left foot is open to the target line, but my knees and shoulders are square to it. An open stance gives the hips a little head start on the downswing and provides a feeling of being "pre-torqued," like a cocked fist or a pistol with the hammer back.

Jack Burke always says, "Your arms should hang like an elephant's trunk"—meaning relaxed, and straight down. I stand fairly close to the ball; I work in a small space. My arms hang naturally. And while my left arm is firm (and the right quite soft), I'm not trying to extend my arms before or during my swing.

The average golfer, on the other hand, stands too far from the ball, his arms outstretched. You can see this vividly with the driver. How often do you see players who are out to hit a hard one creep back farther and farther from the ball and extend their arms until the elbows lock? Perhaps it's a natural instinct, but it doesn't work, because it's moving away from the main power source.

Three things create power in the golf swing: the wrists, the arms, and the body. The body is the most powerful. *The closer your arms are to the body, the closer they are to the power source of the golf swing. The key to long shots is not in the hands, arms, or legs, but in the trunk of the body.* We'll talk more about this in subsequent chapters, but an awareness of this principle is

The Setup

vital in the setup. You must stay close to your power source.

Here's a way to monitor your distance from the ball: Take your address, then simply drop the club. Stay in your stance, and look behind you; if about half the grip extends beyond your heels, you are close enough to the ball. If much less than half the grip protrudes, you're too far away.

DRIVER

DRIVER

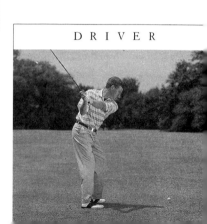

Now I'm ready to **adjust my body**.

Good posture over the ball is as important as anything we do. It feels great to slouch on a couch, but eventually it will be bad for your back. I feel the same way about my setup. A relaxed position is tempting, but bad for golf.

With my feet now set, I bend from the waist to reach the ball and stick my butt out.

I straighten my elbows, then relax them again once or twice. Most observers assume I'm just loosening up, or getting my shirtsleeves out of the way. But what I'm really doing is getting the feeling of attachment of my upper arms to the top of my chest. I'm connecting my arms to the main power source as positively as I can. I want this connection between my arms and my chest because I don't want the arms to work independently; I want them to do what the chest is doing.

Then *I tighten the muscles in my abdomen and rear end.* I haven't shared this point with many people—call it **Elkington's Secret**—but it's vital to my setup and to my attitude about how to hit a ball. By contracting these large muscle groups, there's a live tension in my body that gives me the sensation of being wrapped in, tight. The feeling you want is the one you get when you invite a small child to give you a punch in the stomach and you tighten up.

I look at the target a final time and check my aim. The target should appear slightly to the right of where my mind's eye had been picturing it, definitely not to the left. Why? Because I want to make an aggressive, athletic swing; I want the feeling of swinging out toward my target. The golf swing is under-and-up, and the follow-through is high, toward the target, not under the left shoulder.

The Setup

Finally, just before I hit the ball, **I waggle**. Ideally, this little preparatory movement of the club should be on the same path as the backswing. The point of the waggle isn't rehearsal, however; it's staying in motion. I also move some of the weight in my right foot slightly (and imperceptibly) forward, toward the ball. Then the weight comes right back to the center of the foot. That's basically my forward press, the last thing that happens before I start my backswing. Alex Mercer says I waggle "with intent," that I give every impression of being ready to make a strong swing at my target.

The details of the waggle will vary from player to player. But you need to have some kind of movement.

A stick-figure image of how you should look before you hit the ball would be erect and angular. The head is up; give me enough room between your shoulder and your chest for your left shoulder to fit in! The shoulder should turn under the

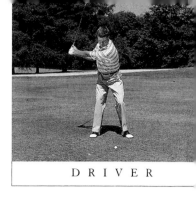

DRIVER

DRIVER

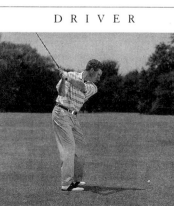

chin at the top of the backswing; Hogan's shirts would fray and rip at that point from repeated contact (chin-shoulder contact can be a useful swing thought and can provide a physical reminder of where your backswing should go).

The knees are bent slightly.

The arms hang straight down, with the elbows in front of the chest, not beside it.

There is a slight bend forward at the waist.

Weight is neither toward the toes or the heels, nor more on the right foot or the left, but central, balanced.

The left shoulder is higher than the right.

The spine is straight, the chest is out, and the butt juts out. If you stand in this position for a while, you will feel some fatigue through the back, hams, and thighs.

Some people might feel awkward in this setup, just as they may feel uncomfortable at first when they grip the club cor-

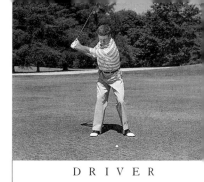

DRIVER

rectly. This feeling won't last. The improvement in your shots will provide a relaxing balm.

There is only one way to make this improvement permanent: practice. Practice your grip, posture, aim, and alignment until you've memorized them and made them a natural part of your routine; then you can "forget" them, and get on with the pleasurable business of hitting strong golf shots, straight at your target.

DRIVER

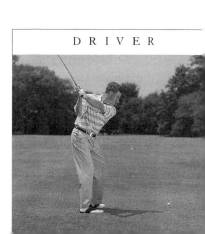

The Setup

FOR THE ADVANCED PLAYER

To me, one of the basic appeals of golf is its naturalness, its lack of regimentation, which gives endless chances for creativity. Unlike baseball, tennis, or football, our field is not level, there are no grids and usually no boundary lines. You're just one person in the middle of 300 acres.

But our vast and endlessly varied playing field leads inevitably to difficulty with aiming. I practice with aim lines and occasionally a competent observer, and get myself dead square. But a month later, I end up too open, with the club too far forward (I never get too closed). The point is, even the best players in the world are constantly adapting.

As the late Jimmy Demaret told me a few months before he died, this difficulty often has a silver lining. Demaret played from a narrow, open stance, and eventually he'd get too narrow and open and start slicing. Then he'd overcorrect, close his setup too much, and start hooking. But in the transition periods between those extremes, he'd play his best golf.

Monitor what your tendencies are, so you can recognize the transition periods. Probably you already know your faults: So many players will say "I've done the same three things wrong my whole life."

The intervals when you're trying to fix something can even happen during your round. Recognize that balls going too far left or too far right are usually the result of an out-of-kilter setup. Be willing to adapt. Then learn how and what to adjust, the way I've learned, the way every good player has learned: through practice.

DRIVER

DRIVER

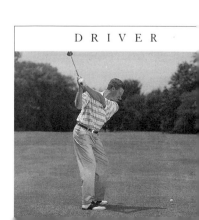

The Setup

◀ Elkington's bag man, Gypsy Joe Grillo, helps his boss
line one up. A friend since he joined the tour in 1987,
Grillo has caddied Elkington to half of his wins on the
Tour. "Gypsy has an up personality and is a virtuoso
caddie. He's as good at his job as I am at mine," says
Elkington. "With all the time we spend together, he
knows me better than anyone—except my wife."

DRIVER

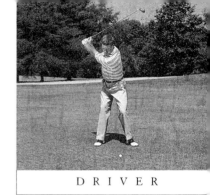

DRIVER

3

———

THE BACKSWING

DRIVER

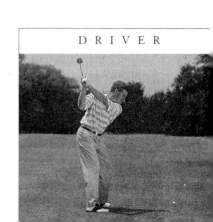

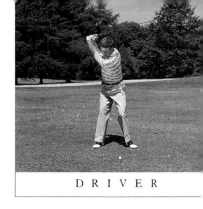

DRIVER

$\mathcal{D}$AVE WILLIAMS WAS right. The Steve Elkington years at the University of Houston were real good, real good. The Cougars won the NCAA Championship in 1984 and 1985, and Elkington, twice an All-American, won the Southwest Conference Championship twice. Elkington also prospered on a personal level. At a fraternity party, he met an attractive Houston native and elementary-education major named Lisa DiStefano. Their relationship solidified during a geography class they took together, and Steve and Lisa married in 1992.

Elkington returned to Australia and turned pro in the fall of 1985.

"A bloke named P.K.—Peter Kennedy—a mate of mine from my hometown and a member of Port Kembla Golf Club, volunteered to caddie for me in my first tournament as a professional down in Tasmania. I gave him the job," Elkington recalls. "Our family has known P.K. forever. He's a wharfie on the docks. Or, as you'd say in the States, P.K.'s a longshoreman. Just a wonderful guy, and as Australian as he can be.

DRIVER

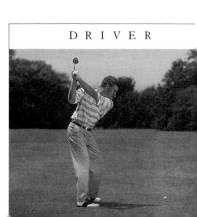

Steve and Lisa Elkington on holiday in Scotland.

"Back then, if I hit a bad shot, I hated myself. I'd go for holes and holes without speaking.

"P.K. didn't take it long. 'Just who the hell do you think you are?' he said. 'Every time we played golf, we had a great time. Now you're trying to do this for a living and you're acting like an idiot. If you don't loosen up and play your game, you're gonna go broke bloody fast and I'll be walking in. And you'd better believe I'll do it.'

"Well, I loosened up a little, and I made a hole in one. And won, of all things, five thousand dollars' worth of blue jeans for it. But I didn't win any money. In fact, I was so low on funds that after the ferry ride back to the mainland I couldn't afford the tickets for us to ride back to Port Kembla on the train. We had to take the bus. Six hundred kilometers, and about thirty-five stops."

P.K., the gap-toothed master of the waterfront, has a story of his own from Elkington's professional debut in the 1985 Tasmanian Open.

"We were walking down the fairway and Steve asks me, 'Did you play cowboys and Indians when you were a kid?' And I wondered, What the hell kind of question is that? and I didn't answer him right away.

"So he asks me again, 'Did you play cowboys and Indians?' I said, 'Of course I did. Every kid does.'

" 'Not me,' he says. 'All I remember is hitting a golf ball.'

"When he won the PGA, he gave me a picture of himself holding the cup. On the picture he wrote 'Cowboys and Indians was never my game.' "

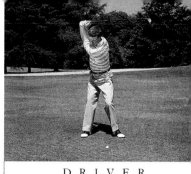

DRIVER

DRIVER

59

Uɴᴛɪʟ ɴᴏᴡ, ᴡᴇ haven't used much of your supply of talent.

If you've got a good grip and setup, half the battle for a powerful, repeating golf swing is won. To a large extent, the club will find its own path.

Half the battle. The other half requires skill and coordination. The backswing represents your first opportunity to use your gift to swing and hit. Talent is required to coordinate the motion of the hands, arms, and body, each of which move on a different plane; there's nothing level in a golf swing. You need skill and experience to decide which and how much of each of these three power sources to use.

My goal in this chapter and the next will be to explain how the power sources work together. I'll discuss the philosophical underpinnings of my swing and look at what several specific body parts are doing, and describe the key constant in the backswing for every shot, regardless of the club or the distance.

The golfer's body could be compared to the space shuttle. The shuttle launch vehicle is a big machine with three main components. The first and most powerful stage, the main booster rocket, is analogous to the golfer's trunk. The secondary booster is the arms. At the top is the orbiter itself, which is the lightest and least powerful part but has the most maneuverability and importance. The shuttle is the wrists, of course.

Spaceships notwithstanding, I'm wary of dissection.

The Backswing

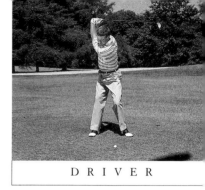

DRIVER

Someone once observed that a golf swing is like a bubble, and if you take away any part of the whole, the bubble bursts. Furthermore, tempo and balance are more important than "correct positions." I've tried to address this problem of emphasis through the inclusion of six flicker swing sequences. By flipping through the photographs, you should be able to sense the rhythm and timing of my swing. Please remember that my physical attributes are unique, as are yours, so don't try to copy my swing too explicitly.

That said, some isolation of the parts of the whole in golf instruction is unavoidable and no doubt necessary. I believe you should know what your component parts do and how they relate to each other, in case something needs to be fixed. You should know your backswing as well as you know your grip and setup, so you can check it out in a second or less. When you throw a soft football pass to a child, you're not thinking about where your right elbow is, or body rotation, are you? Of course not. So unless you're an instructor breaking down a student's swing, or you are working on your swing on the practice tee, focus on targets, not on the position of the left earlobe on the follow-through.

Alex Mercer's response to a question about my tempo is on point: "Most of the ingredients are easy to put a tag on," he said. "Steve has athletic ability, fitness, and strength. But the primary ingredient is mental. Unless you're absolutely sure of the parts of your technique, your mind won't be able to let your rhythm and timing take over."

DRIVER

Before we have a look at those parts, let's jump backward (to the setup) for a moment. One simple rule must be followed: *At address, with the ball comfortably inside your left heel, you must set the center of your body behind the ball.*

The ball is under the left shoulder; the head is positioned well behind the ball.

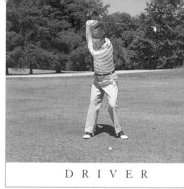

D R I V E R

Why? So that when we turn the shoulder under the chin at the top of the backswing, we'll be in the one and only powerful hitting position: with the head—or the center of the body—behind the ball.

The left shoulder is under the chin, and the right leg is braced. Ready to launch!

Now to the **wrists**.

There's a movement to eliminate the wrists from the modern swing and putting stroke, which is an example of the fads and trendiness in golf instruction that I've avoided all my life.

I think the wrists are as important as anything else in this book.

You need wrist action to hit a ball. What could be more natural? You use your wrists every day for a hundred small

D R I V E R

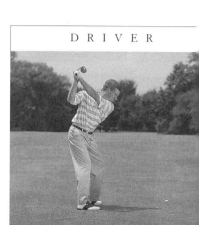

things, from threading a needle to typing on your computer to dealing cards. Although to some, wrist action seems undependable and difficult to time, the wrists are the key to touch and feel, and have been a part of every great golf swing.

So don't take the wrists out; let's learn what their role is so we aren't afraid to use them.

The carpus joints between your forearms and hands should be so relaxed and free that you can move your club back and forth, with the thumbs trying to point to the sky in both directions. If you don't have this freedom in the wrists, your grip is wrong.

The basic action of the wrists is the basic action of the swing: thumbs up to thumbs up.

Alex Mercer always taught me to think of the swing as a mirror image, from thumbs up to thumbs up.

The Backswing

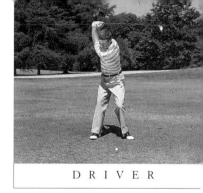

D R I V E R

Their entire range of motion isn't really that great. At a point early in the backswing, try to point the thumbs skyward. Don't delay; blend the wrist break with the backswing motion as the club goes back.

All three power sources start the backswing, each doing its job. The wrists' function is to start to break.

As you can see from the swing sequences, the wrists cock straight up, never to the side. With a correct grip, up and down is the only way the wrists can go.

Every great player in history has cocked his wrists so that the right hand is underneath the club at the top of the backswing.

Now let's talk about the **arms** and what they do.

The arms are the simplest part of the equation. They just follow the torso, with no independent movement of their own. Because the torso is bent from the waist at about a 30-degree angle, and because the arms hang straight down, the

D R I V E R

65

arms swing on an inclined plane. They always react to the chest, because they stay attached to the chest.

The arms have to swing across the body. The left arm has to go under your chin and across the chest. The right arm has to sit underneath the left, as if it were holding it up. Hold the right elbow in close to the torso; the closer you tuck the elbow into your side, the flatter your swing plane will be. The right arm has no independent movement.

Back and forth, from thumbs up to thumbs up. The arms swing as the wrists blend into the up-and-down motion.

As long as the arms make this basic movement, they don't really have to hit certain positions.

Where should the hands be at the top? I'm not dogmatic about this either, as long as they're *somewhere between the right*

The Backswing

shoulder and the ear, and the thumbs are absolutely under the club. My swing plane has gotten flatter over the years—that is, my left arm is lower than it used to be, because I keep my right elbow closer to my rib cage.

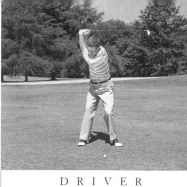

D R I V E R

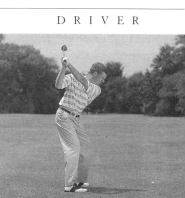

D R I V E R

How far should you take the club back? If you have a good grip, and break your wrists, and keep your arms attached to your torso, I don't care how far back you take it. Unlike most swing students and teachers, I don't think in terms of "parallel" or "past parallel." That smacks of a frozen pose, a position. I think instead of using about 95 percent of my flexibility to get almost as far back as I can. The length of the swing is determined by your ability to turn your left shoulder under your chin.

Which leads us to the **body**, the main power source.

The club starts back, guided not by the arms, hands, or wrists, but by the body. Recall the point I made about the arms feeling connected to the chest. So when I turn my chest, the club goes back exactly where I want it to go—which is slightly inside the target line—because everything is connected to the turning shoulders.

The Backswing

DRIVER

The goal of the backswing is to slam the abdominal muscles into the rib cage. When you've done that, your backswing is finished. This is the key constant in the backswing. Perhaps "slam" is too violent a word; let's instead say *shift the abs back with force every time on a full shot.* This action tells you quite definitely where your backswing ends, and it maximizes the power of your trunk.

Remember the feeling of live tension we talked about in the setup? The backswing is that live tension in motion.

Without moving laterally, the body turns from the waist on the backswing until it can turn no more. Want to hit the ball farther? A quick glance at the longest hitters on the PGA Tour reveals that they're the players who most clearly max out on the turn on the backswing. In other words, they make the most use of the biggest power source—the body—and they move it the fastest.

Of course, it's the unity of their arms, wrists, and body that produces their power, not just their turns. *The key to a really good and efficient swing is that all three of these things—wrists, arms, body—stop at the same time.* You can feel what I feel in my backswing by taking a club and swinging it back. Break your wrists, swing your arms across your chest, turn your upper body to its limit—and stop. You'll have to squeeze your abs to hold this position, even for a second. If you've turned correctly, you're feeling the pent-up energy of torque, the power derived from twisting. You should also be feeling an irresistible urge to hit the hell out of the ball.

DRIVER

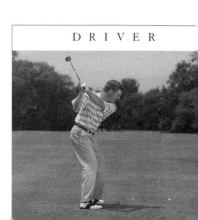

Finally, let's examine the **feet and legs**.

All the things we've done upstairs don't work unless you understand and apply a simple concept: the lever. A lever results from pressure applied at one point to a resisting force at another point. All the leverage you need is in the **right knee.**

One of the most important single things in my golf swing is that *at the top of my backswing, my right knee hasn't moved a single inch from where it was at address.*

The right knee is the anchor to my entire swing. It gives me the stability to make a complete turn, stop, and return powerfully to the ball.

Keeping that knee frozen requires practice and discipline. It also calls for some strength, because the right leg must resist the abs shifting into the right rib cage. Keeping the right knee flexed and braced is not easy; people who say I have an "inactive" lower body don't understand my swing. If you

D R I V E R

grasp the fundamental of leverage, you know that my inactive-appearing lower body is actually resisting just as much as it can.

I've never thought about the left leg in my whole life. From observation I know that as the shoulders turn, the left knee should move back, not up, until it is even with or just to the right of the ball. So the left knee has some movement to it, but far less than some people give it. I'm particularly opposed to lifting the left heel. While going up onto the big toe of the left foot during the backswing may increase the size of the stroke, the player with his heel down will hit more solid shots. My other objection to the high left heel is that it's uncontrollable; few people can gauge how high to lift it each time, or where,

D R I V E R

exactly, the knee will point. Lifting the heel reduces leverage, and thus, power.

How much does the lower body turn on the backswing?

About half as much as the upper body. But never try to add hip turn; if you resist with the right knee, the hips will take care of themselves.

The shoulders move 90 degrees into the center of the body, under the chin; the hips turn about 40; and the knees and lower body turn only about 20. *The lower body is not inactive; it's resistant, especially the right leg.*

BEFORE WE REVIEW what happens in the backswing and put it all together, let's recall two key points about the setup:

1. To ensure that the left shoulder turns under the chin, *your nose and the center of the chest must be behind the ball at address, with the left shoulder high.* In other words, the center of your body must be well behind the ball before you hit it. Behind is where all good shots come from.
2. The left shoulder is a substantial thing, big as a cantaloupe. So you must *hold your head up sufficiently to allow the shoulder to pass under your chin.*

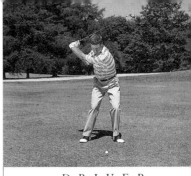

DRIVER

The Backswing

Here are the main components of a good backswing:

- set up with the head and center behind the ball
- waggle with intent
- be sure arms are attached to the chest
- squeeze the abs, part of the live tension in the whole body
- start to cock up the wrists
- turn chest to the right
- shift abs with force into the rib cage

When you can't go back any farther, welcome to the top of the backswing.

DRIVER

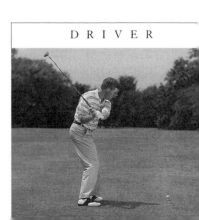

Note my huge shoulder turn and braced right knee. Those two things will help you get an extra twenty.

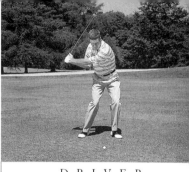

DRIVER

The Backswing

FOR THE ADVANCED PLAYER

How About an Extra Twenty?

Experience has taught you how the three power sources are utilized for various clubs. Short irons require less body; longer irons, knock-downs, and control shots, more arms; and woods, more body. Here's how to prepare to hit a really long shot:

The fundamental way to create more power in the back-swing—and thus, a more powerful shot—is to simply add more tilt to your setup. Raise the left shoulder a little higher; move the ball up toward your left foot slightly, but still comfortably inside the left heel; and move your center back a little farther behind the ball.

And don't forget the essence of the lever, resistance. The right knee must remain firm and flexed.

This powerful position will allow you maximum shoulder turn, while minimizing the arm swing.

DRIVER

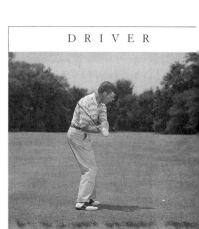

DRIVER

The first tee, final round, the 1995 PGA Championship, at Riviera Country Club, Los Angeles. As predicted by the perfect position of his club at the top, Elkington's three-wood shot finished in the middle of the fairway. He birdied the hole.

DRIVER

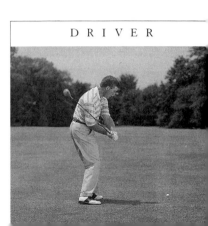

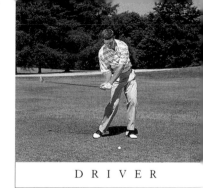

DRIVER

4

———

THE DOWNSWING

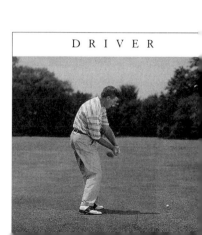

DRIVER

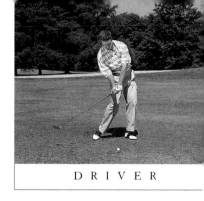

DRIVER

P EARLS AND PARABLES fall from the lips of Jack Burke. "I've seen guys who had perfect swings who couldn't break seventy-five," the sage begins.

"Golf is a *game,* which is a simple fact, but one too many people forget. The people who perform the best are those who like to *play,* not the people who want to win. Everyone wants to win. Michael Jordan loves *playing* his game; Sam Snead would play you up and down the highway for fifty cents."

To support his theory that play—not work—is the true measure of a man, Burke produces a three-page list of quotations he's compiled on the subject. He's an ex-Marine, ex-caddie, ex–professional jock, and he can quote everything from Aristotle to Zen. And he has Steve Elkington's ear.

Burke recalls Shakespeare: "If all the year were playing holidays, / To sport would be as tedious as to work." And the Bible: "The wisdom of a learned man cometh by opportunity of leisure: and he that hath little business shall become wise." Don't play too much; don't work too much.

Elkington turned pro and played for a year in Europe, and

DRIVER

81

Burke watched the young man from Wagga Wagga with interest. Would he develop the playfulness and serenity to complement his obvious competitiveness? Could he adjust during an important round? Could he accept golf's randomness, its bad bounces, and the other guy holing a long putt?

Elkington's talent was such that he qualified for the Tour on his second try and got his card on his twenty-fourth birthday in December 1986. Within three and a half years he was a winner on the Tour, and since 1990 he has averaged a victory a year in some of the biggest tournaments in golf.

The Lakes Golf Club, Sydney, Australia. Elk holds aloft the Stonehaven Cup after winning the 1992 Australian Open.

D R I V E R

And the playfulness Burke talked about? In the final round of the 1997 Players Championship—the "Fifth Major," and a tournament he'd won in 1991—Elkington was nursing a two-shot lead on TPC Sawgrass, one of the scariest courses in golf. As the TV cameras zoomed in and the pressure zoomed up, Elkington played a twenty-yard hook from the middle of the fourteenth fairway. With a nine iron. To eight feet. No uptight mechanical man ever hit such a shot.

"I was 148 yards to a back-left pin, and I knew the ideal shot would be a low, drawing nine iron," says Elkington in a matter-of-fact tone. "My game was in full flow. I wasn't going to back out." (He made the putt and went on to win by seven.)

He finished agonizingly close to the top in two majors in 1995, tying for fifth in the Masters and just two shots out of the playoff for the British Open. After both events he sat in Burke's book-lined, old-leather office at Champions for the usual post-mortems. "You've just had close calls in two major championships and you're expecting to hear some sympathy in his voice, but you know better. He's happy for you, but he's never going to let you be satisfied, certainly not with third place.

"Part of the reason we get on so well is that we've experienced the same things in golf in different eras. We've both had long journeys to get where we are today, and we've survived on fundamentals and toughness. And we've both won majors, something neither of us ever expected to achieve."

Burke, no monologuist, insists on give-and-take. He gets it in spades from Elkington, who once observed from a podium that his caddie had made more money in the previous year than Burke had earned in prize money for his entire career. The old pro got a good laugh from that one.

Burke analyzes Elkington's game: "Steve has what I call 'soft power,' which is like the ballet dancer who can catch that

D R I V E R

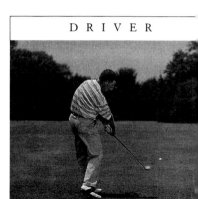

woman who weighs 110 pounds and do it with grace. You don't see anything stiff, calculated, or jerky in his swing. He has very long arms, so he can make a big circle that develops a lot of power. People call it effortless, but it's a well-thought-out, well-contrived circle he makes.

"In college, he was too quick to hit a putt, too quick to hit a shot. People who do that make a lot of mistakes, but he's slowed down a lot over the years, and has gotten a certain rhythm on the greens that you need to be good at putting. I may have had some influence on that.

"But what I really like about Steve is that he's a very perceptive person, and he's always learning. He can curve the ball, play any shot that's needed. He's one of the few guys out there who really play the game."

The Downswing

D R I V E R

Everything I've said in this book is of equal importance. A fundamentally correct golf swing is the result of a distinct chain of events, and any weak link can destroy the whole. Just as a sound setup is impossible without a good grip, the principles of the backswing must be observed to make an efficient and powerful downswing.

We've discussed the first three fundamentals: grip, setup, and backswing. With those building blocks in place, we can now examine what happens in the downswing, and why.

Throughout my life in golf, I've found that if I understood a particular move I could do it, that with practice I could incorporate it into my swing. And when I began to grasp the sequence of things, I could practice anything I wanted with concentration but no confusion, because I knew how everything fit.

With all the fundamentals of grip, posture, and backswing in place, the end of the swing sequence, the downswing, has a certain inevitability. (See photo, page 86.)

At the top of the backswing, the right knee has held its flex, the abdominal muscles have been shifted into the right rib cage until they can go no farther, the left shoulder is under the chin, and the center of the body is positioned well behind the ball. (See photo, page 87.)

From this position, the downswing begins. It has two parts. The first part begins with the moment the backswing becomes the downswing. This is called the transition.

This part of the swing is vitally important. I like to think of it as the timing portion of the swing. Everything's wound up

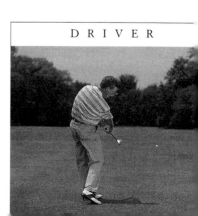

D R I V E R

and ready to explode on the ball—but we need a bit of patience first.

Because the shoulders have to travel the farthest on the backswing—90 degrees, compared to 40 degrees for the hips and 20 degrees for the knees—they must be given a little head start in the unwinding process before we turn on the full jets. *That is why I pause my hips and knees slightly, allowing the shoulders to move more quickly than the hips or the torso.* This is what I call getting into the **stacked position**, when shoulders, hips, and knees are all turned about the same amount. (See photo, page 88.)

This portion of the swing may be the most difficult to master, but it's not particularly hard to understand.

During this first, critical part of the downswing, the club has to go into free fall. The club looks and feels to be falling straight

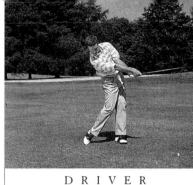

D R I V E R

down. *The key is to get the feeling of pushing your weight straight down, into both feet.* This allows the shoulders to unwind a little bit, while balancing you enough to make a powerful turn through the ball.

The shaft of the club is parallel to the ground and to the target line at this point, and is poised to deliver the blow. The wrists have held their position; they have not uncocked. Both feet are flat on the ground. The hips and knees are doing nothing. The left shoulder has turned enough to catch up with the other power sources. The spine is still tilted to the right, which gives you the inside path to hit the inside of the ball. (See photo, page 89.)

D R I V E R

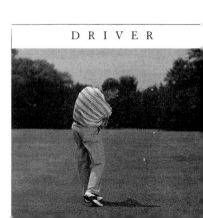

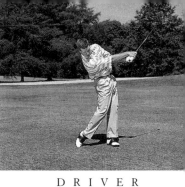

DRIVER

DRIVER

You've reached the stacked position, the second part of the downswing. Now we can turn on the power. As the club head approaches the ball, the left leg begins to straighten, and the trunk clears to the left as fast as you want it to. This unwinding of the torso squares up the club face and shoots the club into the ball, not any independent movement of the hands or the arms.

Please note that in the transition, when the club begins its

free fall, the abdominal muscles simultaneously start to pull to the left. This will help to pull you around to the finish. This use of the abs will also help you acquire good rhythm.

And the legs? The right leg is moving in unison with the shifting of the abdominal muscles. The right foot rolls into the left side of the shoe, and is pulled up onto the big toe at the finish by the force of the unwind. The left leg is straightening.

After you've hit the ball, and the hips, abs, torso, and shoulder have turned the corner, the left leg continues to straighten.

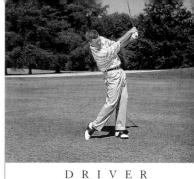

DRIVER

DRIVER

Building your downswing in the way I've described will require understanding, coordination, talent, and, above all, practice.

A few big-picture thoughts:

The downswing is a release of the torque in the upper body and of the resistance below. My downswing is tight, with no slack and just a touch of lateral movement. With practice, no particular thoughts will be required to make the return half of the swing, except for that familiar one of keeping your eye on the back of the ball.

As long as you maintain your focus on a spot on the back of the ball, I don't think you need to think at all about keeping your head still. The eyes will keep your head behind the ball

DRIVER

in a little pocket I call the hitting zone. Think about your eyes, in other words, not your head.

The secret to my swing, if there is one, is that it has no slack, no dipping. It's a simple swing, with no forced movement. It's one torso move, from the head to the legs. I have a feeling of being encased, as if I'm a spinning steel cylinder, anchored at both ends. Despite this book's necessary isolation and dissection of the parts of the swing, it's all one swing.

The downswing is a one-piece pulling sensation, with the pull supplied by the spinning torso and hips. The right foot must *roll* into impact, with only the inside of the shoe touching the ground.

Here's a thought that may help on your downswing: Imagine the pent-up energy of the backswing as an agitated can of spray paint. You don't want to release the pressure all at once and have the can's contents spray all over. Instead, you ease off the pressure gradually. You do this in your downswing by gently rolling onto the instep of the right foot, then up to the toes. This image might help you slow down your arm speed, allowing you to hit the ball with all your power sources.

DRIVER

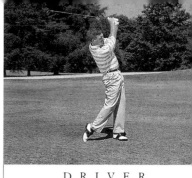

The Downswing

LET'S REVIEW THE basics of the downswing:

Phase One

■ Since the shoulders have turned so much farther than the hips and the knees, and since they have the longest distance back to the ball, you must unwind the shoulders about 40 degrees while the other parts remain relatively stationary.

■ Both feet remain flat, as you get the feeling of pushing your weight through the feet and into the ground.

■ During this pause in hip and knee action, the club is in free fall, and the left shoulder is returning toward the address position.

■ The entire right foot must remain flat, as if your weight is pushing it into the ground.

■ You've reached the proper position when you're "stacked"— the shoulders, hips, and knees are all turned the same distance from the ball, and the shaft of the club is parallel to the target line.

Phase Two

■ Clear the left hip.

■ Your eyes remain focused on the back of the ball.

■ Your head has remained in the hitting zone, which allows the right shoulder to pass underneath the chin, while . . .

■ Straightening the left leg.

■ Once you've reached the stacked position, clear everything to the left.

D R I V E R

95

If you were to check your swing on video, these are the reference points you would use.

DRIVER

THE PLANE TRUTH

In the 1957 classic instruction book *Five Lessons,* Ben Hogan and artist Anthony Ravielli produced their famous image of the swing plane as an imaginary plate of glass, resting on the golfer's shoulders as it leans on its edge from the ball.

This is a useful image, because it provides a road map to help you swing back and through on the same path.

But there has been a good deal of confusion regarding the swing plane, because many instructors have presented it as a goal in itself, and the key to golf. It is neither. The target is and always will be the goal. The swing plane is a reference point, second in importance to the target line.

While I'm well known for my rhythm and tempo, these (and the back cover) photos illustrate that I hit the correct positions relative to both the swing plane and the target line. Take some time to examine these pictures so you will understand the meaning of the lines we golfers are always drawing in the air.

DRIVER

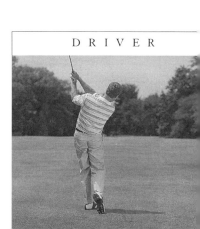

The shaft is parallel to the ground and parallel to the target line.

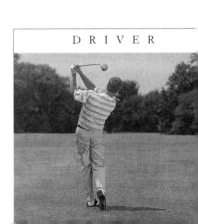

DRIVER

The left arm is parallel to the ground. The butt end of the
club points to the target line.

DRIVER

The one and only time the shaft touches the plane line.

The left arm is parallel to the ground, and the butt end of the club points to the target line.

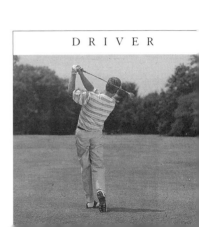

DRIVER

DRIVER

The shaft is parallel to the ground and parallel to the target line.

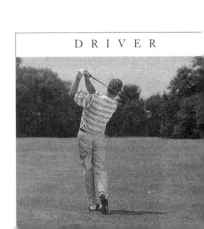

DRIVER

Impact. Notice that the hands and the shaft are much higher than they were at address.

DRIVER

The right arm is approximately parallel to the ground; the butt end of
the club points to the target line.

The right arm is on the plane line.

Next page:
six iron

Next page:
sand bunker

FOR THE ADVANCED PLAYER

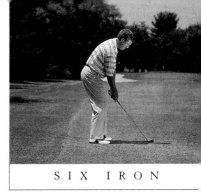

SIX IRON

The Governor

We've learned that there are three power sources: the wrists, the arms, and the body. Here's a fourth, the right foot. Use it when playing control shots, especially spinning wedge shots, when you need to take some of the body out of the shot.

Actually, the right foot in this case is less a power source than a governor, more a brake than an accelerator.

When I want to hit a low shot with a wedge, with lots of spin and precisely controlled distance, I don't come up onto my right toe on the follow-through as I would for a normal full shot. This is because I don't need the full thrust from my biggest power source, the body. Instead, I roll onto my right foot and ankle on the downswing, and I don't permit the right heel to rise more than an inch or two at the finish. This restricts the hip turn, which in turn makes me cock my wrists up, which stops my arms from flying away.

Back in my college days, I was the worst wedge player there ever was. That's what had me practicing every morning in the field at Hofheinz Pavilion. I thought that just by repetition I'd get better. But my problem wasn't lack of effort; it was poor understanding of technique.

I never got the image of proper wedge play until I watched Lee Trevino in the Houston Open in about 1983. The lights really came on for me when I saw the way he controlled a variety of wedge shots by using a score of variations on the right foot governor.

SAND BUNKER

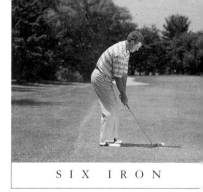

SIX IRON

◀ A classic photo, circa 1960, of John Joseph Burke, Jr. "I love this picture," says Elkington. "Look at Jack's eyes, and his head position, and his right shoe, and how the right arm is under the left. And check out the pack of Lucky Strikes in his back pocket."

SAND BUNKER

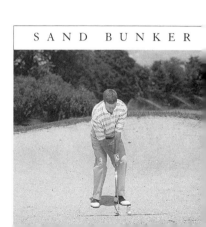

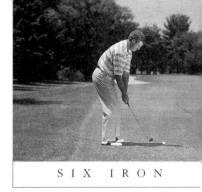

SIX IRON

5

——

RHYTHM
AND TEMPO

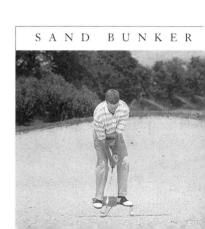

SAND BUNKER

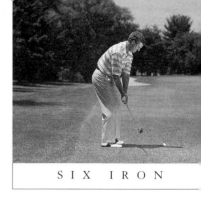

THE FINAL ROUND of the PGA Championship, August 13, 1995, Riviera Country Club, Pacific Palisades, California: Harsh sunlight burned through the early-morning fog in the canyons near Sunset Boulevard, and Riviera, for seventy years the golf and polo playground for Hollywood's royalty, almost couldn't take it. All week the course had baked in the summer heat, and the recently replanted greens were turning brown. Spike marks in the sensitive turf loomed like pinball bumpers to some frustrated players. But Steve Elkington hardly noticed; he was seeing targets, not obstacles.

On the tenth, possibly the best and trickiest short par four in golf, Elkington had used his "governor" shot for his approach to the green. From fifty yards out, his quickly spinning wedge danced on the green as if an underground magnet were pulling it toward the flagstick. The ball stopped two feet from the hole. He tapped it in, his growing gallery shouted, he tipped his hat stoically. Incredibly, he'd made up six shots on leader Ernie Els in ten holes. With his birdie on ten, his fifth of the day, he'd tied Els for the lead.

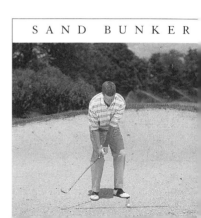

Elkington glanced at the scoreboard near the tenth green and watched as −15 scrolled up opposite his name. And then, for an instant, he saw another number on the board, a 72-hole score: −17.

Was this a vision—or too much sun? Seventeen under par would be a record for the PGA Championship (by three shots) and would equal Greg Norman's record (in the 1993 British Open) for the lowest total ever for a major championship. Moreover, for Elkington to reach –17 would require a 64, the lowest-ever final round to win a PGA. Even under perfect conditions, the final six holes at Riviera are difficult, demanding heroic iron shots from the player hunting birdies. But Elkington believes in premonitions, and that an impulsive, unpredictable golf god decides the winners in the majors. Was that his hand on Elkington's shoulder?

Rhythm and Tempo

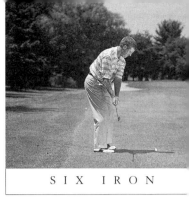

SIX IRON

You may have purchased this book to get some insight into the tempo and balance in my golf swing. Addressing those issues now is not a matter of saving the best for last, but of discussing things in sequence. I simply could not talk about this all-encompassing fundamental before you'd considered the basics of grip, setup, backswing, and downswing. While rhythm is always a good thing to think about, if other parts of your game have serious flaws, adding rhythm to a bad swing is like painting over the rust spots on your car.

If you've read carefully and you've flipped through the flicker swing sequences, then you've probably discovered the seeming paradox of my golf swing. The rhythm and tempo for which I'm well known are not a product of a relaxed body and a gentle grip, as you may have thought; I very definitely contract the muscles in my hands and my torso when I set up and when I hit. And while my swing appears to be smooth and uncomplicated, it is, in fact, an intricate thing. I certainly wasn't born with it.

I've also taken pains to tell you that a rhythmic swing depends in large part on your state of mind. You must be confident of the other fundamentals to swing freely and with grace. Now that we've discussed those other basics, we're ready to talk about the fifth fundamental.

Tempo relates to a person's manner or style, which may be fast or slow or in-between. You're born with a certain tempo for doing things, but slow walking or talking does not always mean slow swinging. I happen to be quite an energetic person, and my mind often races a mile a minute, but no one would describe my swing as fast. Nick Price is the opposite, a man with a very brisk tempo on the course, and a slow pace off it.

SAND BUNKER

Greg Norman is an example of a golfer whose up-tempo swing matches his personality.

Tempo, in other words, is part of your personal style. It's a pace of doing things you bring to the table, and it would be fruitless to try to change it. Obviously, a variety of golf swing tempos can succeed.

Rhythm is different. For our purposes, I'll define it as *repetition of the fundamentals at a beat.* The beat is crucial for timing, because it leads to consistent hitting of the center of the ball with the center of the club face.

Unlike tempo, rhythm can be taught, and learned. Alex Mercer, my first coach, emphasized rhythm in every lesson. Look closely at what he has to say about my swing.

> Steve's excellent rhythm comes from his ability to swing the club in an almost musical way, getting the beats and the timing down every time. There's no doubt a huge amount of his strength comes from the leverage he gets from his lower body. That's why he can hit it so far without seeming to try very hard.

Alex's comment holds the key: Consistently good rhythm can occur only when the grip and setup are correct and comfortable, and the important points of backswing and downswing are observed.

Your job is to do all the fundamentals at your speed. If you can do the job quickly, fine, that's your rhythm. The object is to create a blueprint, one or two or a series of checkpoints. For example, I make a goal of completing my backswing. I think about going all the way back, and all the way through, because when my rhythm is off, almost invariably it's because I'm not completing my backswing. When I'm playing well, I have a clear picture in my mind of what I have to do on my backswing.

But we've all seen mechanically good players who looked, well, mechanical. Correct fundamentals aren't the entire story; the rhythm in my swing comes from a variety of things.

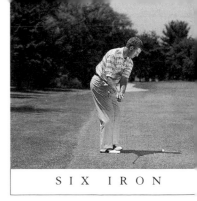

S I X   I R O N

First of all, *I am an athlete.* I've been blessed with balance and touch. I can throw a ball or catch one, and I can hit a moving ball, too. My snooker game is quite above average. The point is, if you can't dance or assume the basic athletic position from another sport, finding a balanced, graceful golf swing won't be easy for you. Golf is a sport, it relates to other sports, and we shouldn't pretend the nonathlete will have an easy time with it.

For example, I've spoken of the live, springy tension I feel in my setup and grip, and of the great resistance of the lower body to the shoulder and chest turn at the top of the backswing. As you know, I tighten my abs before I swing. I shift these muscles forcefully to the right on the backswing, and shift them again in the opposite direction on the downswing. *A swing that relies on the torso, the biggest power source, will be more rhythmic.* Why? Because moving the abs all the way to the right, then all the way to the left, provides the boundaries for the swing. Turning the left shoulder to the center of the body—and then back—does the same thing. Without definite margins, the swing becomes haphazard, a matter of day-to-day guesswork. And there's no grace in a guess.

The torso is not the only thing that produces a good tempo; the entire body is involved. *Flexibility* is a key part of the equation. I am extremely flexible. To get a good hamstring stretch before I play golf with friends, I'll often throw a leg onto the roof of a golf cart. I can touch my palms to the floor without bending my knees, which speaks not only to my limberness but also to the

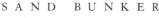

S A N D   B U N K E R

length of my arms. I can't buy off the rack; all my dress shirts are custom-made. Long arms are a definite asset to the golfer.

Without question, I was built for this game.

WHILE YOU CAN'T expect to grow longer arms, there are some things you can do to improve your rhythm. And the first of these is to *build your strength*. After reading this far into the book, you shouldn't be surprised that my workouts focus on my abdominals and on the muscles in my back and legs.

As you can see from the photos in the appendix, crunches and medicine balls are the keys to my ab work. I do my crunches with my hands crossed on my chest, not linked behind my neck. I do a variety of drills with medicine balls weighing up to 16 pounds. One exercise my bookish coauthor couldn't handle involves catching the heavy ball while lying supine, with the hands above the head, then sitting up to hand the ball to the workout partner.

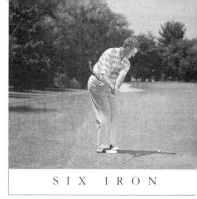

SIX IRON

EQUIPMENT

Another way to build a good rhythm in your swing requires a bit of heavy lifting. When people admire my swing and ask me how I do it, I say "First of all, I've got nice *heavy equipment*." I find it much easier to swing smoothly with weight. Heavier clubs are a crucial part—perhaps the most crucial part—of rhythmic swinging. My clubs weigh enough that I'm more or less forced to swing "with a beat." I can lose that music in one or two swings with a too-light club, because I lose track of where the club head is. One of the secrets of the game is knowing precisely where the club head is, a technique that's harder to master with light clubs. Which would you rather swing, a hammer or a feather?

But the golf-equipment industry is in the throes of a fad to give you ever-lighter clubs with ever-longer shafts. But light, long clubs are harder to control and more difficult to swing in rhythm. In the old days, 13½ ounces was the standard dead-weight of a driver. Now it's 11 ounces, even 10. That's too light.

I know what the argument will be: lighter club, faster club-head speed, longer shots. For one club only, the driver, I'll go along, a bit reluctantly. Distance off the tee is so important to so many people, and I won't try to stand in the way. But for the other clubs, where your target may be a twenty-foot-wide section of green instead of a forty-yard-wide fairway, I strongly suggest you investigate the benefits of weight.

The overall weight of my five iron is 15½ ounces; the typical modern five iron weighs an ounce or two less. You can see we're not talking about that much weight, no more than that of a small saltshaker. So don't let the latest trend in the golf industry sway you. Use a bit more weight, not a little less.

SAND BUNKER

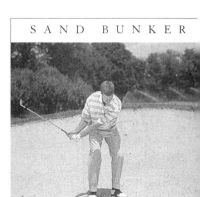

My clubs are some of the heaviest on the Tour, and my rhythm and tempo are among the best. I have no doubt there is a connection.

My specs: The swingweight of my Titleist forged blades is D-5. My irons are bent one degree flat, and all my clubs are one-half inch shorter than the new, ever-lengthening "standard" (my two iron, for example, is 39 inches long, and my three iron is $38\frac{1}{2}$ inches; my irons get shorter in half-inch increments). The shafts in my irons are steel Dynamic Gold X-100s. My three wood, a 13-degree Titleist PT, has a metal head and a steel shaft. My driver, also a Titleist, is 44 inches long, has 9 degrees of loft, and is the only graphite shaft in my bag. As I mentioned earlier, I use Eaton Golf Pride Victory Cord grips.

Why am I so particular about my clubs? Because correct equipment, tempo, and rhythm are so interrelated that I don't believe you can have any one without the other two.

After you get some proper equipment, I recommend that you make a record of your clubs's lengths, lofts, lies, and weights. Soon after I won the PGA, my clubs were stolen from the trunk of my car in a restaurant parking lot. I hadn't noted the exact specs of my clubs; as a result, every set I tried for the next six months felt a bit funny to me. Like most top players, you can hand me a club and I can guess within a half ounce that club's weight, and within a quarter of an inch its length. I now have clubs that suit me, and a record of my specs under lock and key.

I run into amateur golfers all the time who will tell me, "I never missed a fairway with my old driver" or "I have a three wood at home that I really love." When you have a favorite club like that, my advice is to measure it, weigh it, and try to duplicate it. Or in most cases, use it!

Rhythm and Tempo

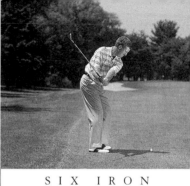

S I X   I R O N

Today's golf equipment can be so expensive that I further recommend that you take the five hundred dollars you've saved to buy a new driver and spend it instead on ten lessons. If you've saved a few thousand for an entire set, invest instead in lessons for yourself and for your kids. And get your kids some old, inexpensive clubs to learn with.

ONE OF THE biggest challenges a golfer faces today is finding good equipment that fits. Golf has had an amazing growth spurt in recent years—and a corresponding growth in clubs that aren't even fit to stir a fire.

Your equipment can make you or break you, not only in terms of your rhythm, which we just discussed, but in how high and how far you hit the ball, and in what curve you put on it. Incorrect lies, lofts, grips, and lengths can make a hard game even harder.

Club makers build things into your game in several ways, especially in the irons, without your even knowing it. There are three basic looks in the irons: square, semi-goosed, and goosed ("goosed" is Australian for offset, meaning the club face is bent back from the butt end of the shaft). Most traditional forged irons are square; the Titleist DCI is a semi-offset club, and Pings are fully goosed. The more goose you have, the higher you will hit the ball and the more you will hook. Every degree of offset equates to a degree of hook in the sky. Obviously, a golfer who normally hooks his shots wouldn't play with a fully goosed set of irons.

Another way equipment attempts to adjust your ball flight is with the shaft. Believe me, there are more types of shafts out there today than candy in a candy shop. Some shafts torque more than others (we're talking primarily about graphite here;

S A N D   B U N K E R

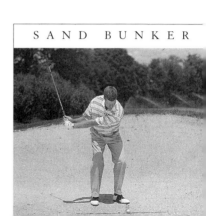

121

steel shafts have practically zero torque). Some shafts are manu-factured with as much as 10 degrees of torque, which trans-lates to 10 degrees of hook in the sky (each degree of torque equals 1 degree of hook in the air). To feel what torque is, hold a club by the grip with one hand and by the head with the other hand. Now twist.

Another shaft characteristic you should be aware of is kick point. The kick point is the spot on the shaft that flexes the most when you hit a ball. A high kick point, up near the grip, makes the ball go low. Just the opposite for a low kick point. Between torque and offset, you could have as much as 18 or 20 degrees of hook in the sky built into your clubs. There's a mind-boggling array of shafts on the market with endless combinations of flex, torque, and kick point, making it quite difficult to pick what's right for you.

Try to find a simple set of golf clubs. I don't believe in com-pensating for a fault with my clubs; you're better off fixing the swing. As Jack Burke says, "I don't want messages built into my equipment." Better players, and those who aspire to be bet-ter, want a plain vanilla set. We'll do the rest with our talent, touch, and technique. We'll decide what spin to use, and how to adjust the height and distance. To me, that's a big part of the fun of our game.

Before we leave equipment, I'd like to say a word about shoes. I don't like plastic cleats. I do like heavy leather shoes with metal spikes. I want my feet in the ground; I want to feel anchored. If they made shoes with longer spikes, I'd wear them, because then I could build more torque and leverage in my swing.

You couldn't swing like me if your feet left the ground. The great instructor Claude Harmon had a saying for poorly anchored golfers who hit wild shots: "It's like shooting a cannon from a canoe."

Unfortunately, metal spikes can damage greens when the ignorant or inconsiderate wearer doesn't lift his feet when he walks. This has led to the banning of metal on more and more courses.

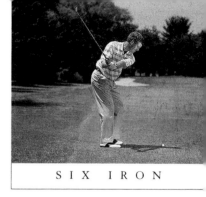

SIX IRON

Eᴌᴋɪɴɢᴛᴏɴ ʜᴀᴅ ʙᴇᴇɴ hooking the ball for months.

But he realized that the right-to-left curve that had been so useful at The Masters and at the British Open on the Old Course at Saint Andrews was the wrong shot for the PGA. Riviera responded best to a fade. And as Jimmy Demaret had predicted, there was beauty in the transition. After Elkington practiced hitting slices, he arrived at Riviera hitting a Hogan-like "bullet fade."

He came to the eleventh hole, a 564-yard journey over a wide barranca and through a tunnel of overhanging eucalyptus trees. Even the longest hitters in the world seldom reach this green in two, and most don't even try. But after driving well, the tournament coleader took the three wood from his bag. The tall, fragrant trees and the greenside bunker were invisible to him. He saw only his target, the flagstick, 280 yards in the distance.

The TV announcer in his canopied tower murmured into his microphone, while a cameraman scurried into the fairway to catch the moment. Elkington, oblivious, went through his routine: left-hand grip, visual check of the grip, target check, right-hand grip, and a little half practice swing. He walked to the ball with his right shoulder low and took his stance, setting up with the ball forward a fraction, his left shoulder slightly higher than usual: the kill shot.

SAND BUNKER

He killed it. The ball finished dead on line, six steps from the front edge. A chip from the kikuyu and an eight-foot putt gave Elkington his sixth birdie of the day, and, remarkably, the lead.

Wanting a low fade for his tee shot on the next hole, the tight, right-bending twelfth, Elkington opened his stance slightly and moved the ball a fraction back in his stance. He had a feeling of "holding on" with his left hand through the hitting area, which produced a gentle, drifting fade into the fairway, 162 yards from the hole.

The twelfth green at Riviera perches on an uninviting little plateau. It's protected on the left by a deep, oval bunker and on the right by Bogey's Tree, a tall sycamore that often shaded actor Humphrey Bogart. Back in the old days, Hollywood's favorite leading man liked to sit in the sun-dappled shade and watch the Los Angeles Open, accompanied by Lauren Bacall, a pack of cigarettes, and a thermos bottle of bourbon.

Elkington's second to the twelfth would have brought Bogey to his feet: a soft, cut seven iron to within nine feet of the nearly inaccessible back right pin. He made the putt for his third birdie in a row, his seventh birdie of the day.

"My iron play was so good, I didn't see any point in shooting away from the flags," Elkington said ninety minutes later. "In fact, I did the opposite. Something inside me was saying 'You've got to shoot at the flags, you've got to keep attacking.' So I kept the hammer down all the way in."

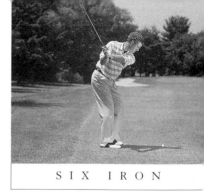

SIX IRON

I'D LIKE TO end with a bit of my thinking on the mental side of golf.

Jack Burke always says that golf is a five-hour examination of your skills. First, you have to execute, and second, execute with the right plan.

All sportsmen play best when in the same frame of mind— thinking only of targets. The second-best thing to think about: nothing. When you've got your mind right, there's no fear or pressure.

If you're really competing, mechanics should not enter your mind. When Larry Bird attempted a three-point shot, he certainly wasn't thinking about his grip or his elbow position or which way his feet were pointed. When Joe Montana lofted a soft past down the sidelines to a sprinting Jerry Rice, neither the quarterback nor the receiver had to think about how to accomplish the task. They'd done that in practice. To a great degree your golf shots should be as planned and executed as the practiced moves in any other sport.

A case in point for me came at the 1989 Shearson Lehman Hutton Open in San Diego. I led by two after three rounds, but I didn't win. Four times during that round I hit balls over greens by going aggressively at protected flagsticks. As Jack Burke helped me realize later, I should have been going for the center of some of those greens, then allowing my putter to go to work. When I began to win on Tour, it was mostly with off-the-rack shots, not heroic ones.

When it's all said and done, how do you know if you played as well as you could? I don't think the score alone gives you the answer. I like to apply this test: If you made a decision on each shot, if you chose a target and a club each time, and if you

SAND BUNKER

cleared your mind and swung freely at the target, then you've done as well as you can.

Those few things should be enough to occupy anyone's attention on the golf course. I don't have any space for rent in my mind for negative thoughts.

At Riviera during the '95 PGA I had no particular thoughts, no big conversations with myself. I knew I was in a big arena, but I was just numb to it. I felt as if I were in the eye of a hurricane. I let all the pressure out of me, and let the press and the crowd and the people watching on television have it.

I'm like the basketball player who wants the ball at the end of the game. I feel that all my work's been done, and I can get down to just competing. I'm not anxious about how things will turn out.

"TAILS, MR. ELKINGTON," the PGA official said. "You have the honor."

The vision had become real: Elkington shot 64 in the suffocating pressure of the final round of the PGA, and had set or broken a handful of records. But he hadn't won the tournament. Colin Montgomerie had played spectacularly, too, and now they were playing off at sudden death for the title.

The competitors arrived at the eighteenth, perhaps the best hole on a very good golf course. The tee shot is partially blind, uphill, and framed on the right by eucalyptus trees and on the left by a hill. Both players hit bullets into the fairway, and faced shots of about 170 yards to the smallish, perched green. Both hit adrenaline-fueled eight irons onto the wilting grass of the half-amphitheater of the green. The crowd stood, overheated and overexcited, and gave the players a standing ovation. Elkington and Montgomerie trudged silently up the hill, their faces masks shining with sweat, and pressure, and the excitement of the moment.

Elkington's ball had hit his target, the center of the green, twenty feet from the hole, in the exact spot where Montgomerie had holed a half hour earlier to force the playoff. Elkington had watched the putt on a TV monitor in the clubhouse. He'd thrown his bottle of water against the wall when the Scotsman's ball went in, but he'd also noted the exact path the ball had taken to the hole. Here was the perceptiveness and awareness of the elite performer. "Look, look, look," Elkington often repeats to himself when he's in a competition.

Now Montgomerie's ball lay eighteen feet from the hole, closer than Elkington's, but on a more difficult line.

The Australian putted first.

Putter hit ball in the hush—*click*—and the shouts began as the ball rolled through the alternating bands of green and brown. Pandemonium broke out when the ball went in. Elkington raised his hands above his head, his eyes shut, his teeth bared. A minute and a half later, Montgomerie putted and missed.

"It's almost something you don't want to talk about," he said a few minutes later. "It's such a personal thing, you can't explain it, you can't even explain it to your wife, what you were doing."

Something Alex Mercer said comes back when you watch the tapes of the 1995 PGA. "Golf is an art," the wise old pro often said. "And Steve is an artist." If that is so, the inspiration to win at golf must be like the creative impulse to the artist: a visitor, not a captive. A thing not ordered or owned, but awaited, prepared for.

Elkington was ready.

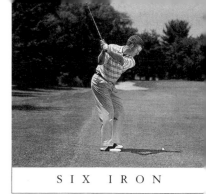

SIX IRON

SAND BUNKER

THE SHORT GAME

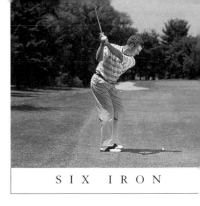

SIX IRON

CHIPS AND PITCHES

This is a book about the swing, but it is also about golf. And that compels me to address that crucial aspect of our sport called the short game.

No lectures from me about the importance of the short ones; you already know that every shot counts one. So let's look at several of the fundamentals of chipping every player should master.

The first rule is this: You must select the spot on the green or the fringe where you want your chip to land. This will determine what club you use.

The second rule: Nearly all chips and pitches should be played with most of the weight on the left foot. This ensures a descending blow.

I learned two chipping methods from Alex Mercer when I was a kid, and I've stuck with them. The first of these, which I call **The Y**, is very dependable for the pitch-and-run. It's

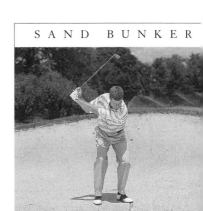

SAND BUNKER

quite simple: Get the weight forward, where it belongs, then make the letter Y with your arms and the club. The goal is to keep the Y uniform throughout the stroke. Hit the ball without breaking the wrists, and power the stroke by lowering the left shoulder on the backswing and raising it on the downswing. It's almost a putting stroke. The Y is not a powerful shot. Use it for low, running chips within about thirty yards of the green.

For the higher shots around the green, I use what I call the **Break and Lock,** or the **Break/Don't Break.** This method is powered by the shoulders primarily, with a very small hip rotation. Break or cock the wrists on the backswing, then power them forward with the shoulders and hips without uncocking on the downswing or even after the hit; the right hand should never pass the left.

Compared to the shoulders in the full swing, the shoulders in the Break and Lock swing turn a little more parallel to the ground. This gives the club a shallower path and ensures good, crisp contact.

What club should you use? My philosophy is to pick the spot where I want the ball to land, then choose one of the fourteen. You should use the least-lofted club that will land the ball comfortably on the green, then let the ball roll to the hole. The rule of thumb on running chips is to fly the ball one-third of the distance and allow two-thirds for roll; for lofted shots, fly the ball two-thirds of the distance to the hole and allow one-third for roll.

I'll chip with anything to get the job done, not just the wedges. I practice the basic chipping methods with almost every club in the bag. I'll even use a three wood from the fringe, and chip the ball with a putting motion.

FOR THE ADVANCED PLAYER

When I want a shallower stroke for lofted shots, I work the shoulders. Unlike the full swing, where the shoulders go under and up, I often want my shoulders to work parallel to the ground for high, soft shots near the green. As in the Break and Lock, this makes for a shallower stroke and more solid contact.

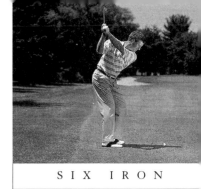

SIX IRON

SAND BUNKER

1

2

5

6

3

4

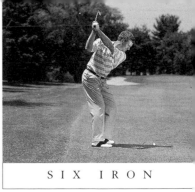

SIX IRON

7

8

SAND BUNKER

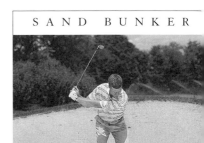

1

2

5

6

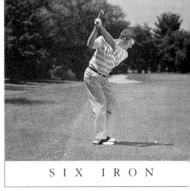

3

4

7

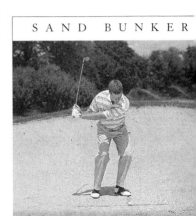

8

SAND BUNKER

SAND PLAY

As with chips and pitches, sand play requires an understanding of technique, then a good deal of practice.

The shot from the bunker needs to be an aggressive stroke. Enough sand should exit the bunker to fill a coffee cup, which can't be accomplished with a mere flick of the wrists.

As you can see in the sand-bunker swing sequence, I've drawn a line in the sand opposite the big toe of my left foot. *This is the only place from which to hit good bunker shots.* With the ball that far forward, your hands are naturally well back behind the ball.

If I put you in the practice fairway in this setup, you'd probably say, "I can't do this. I'll hit it fat"—which is precisely the idea. You don't have to hit the ball to get out of a greenside bunker; you hit the sand behind it and underneath it. So we want you to hit this shot "fat"—that is, to hit behind the ball.

I'm always asked how far I hit behind the ball. Your club should enter the sand close to the ball for long shots and farther from the ball for short ones. The simplest and best way to control how far behind the ball to enter the sand is to match that distance to the distance you hold the hands behind the ball. In other words, if the hands are ten inches behind the ball, your club will enter the sand ten inches "fat." Obviously, for a long bunker shot you'd hold your hands not very far behind the ball.

How do you hit it? What is the swing motion? Good questions, because we are in fact hitting the ball fat, requiring a technique different from that for shots from grass.

The right arm is the key. Take a normal backswing, but on the downswing release the right arm early by straightening the right wrist just before and during impact. The right wrist

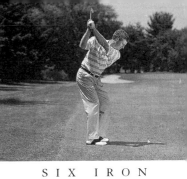

SIX IRON

SAND BUNKER

137

should go under the left hand. It's a wristy, throwing motion with the right hand. If you held the right wrist angle, as you would with a chip shot, you'd risk hitting the ball clean—and clear over the green.

Understanding the swing is the key in the bunker; as long as you put the ball opposite the left foot, don't worry too much about the setup. Claude Harmon, one of the greatest sand players in history, often said he didn't care where you put your feet as long as your motion was correct. I think a little open stance is good, but I have never felt you have to swing outside and cut across to be effective.

The basic swing motion for the greenside bunker is what I call a reverse swing. For a normal shot off the tee or from grass, the club goes inside, then along the swing plane, and back to inside as you finish your swing. But the bunker swing feels just the opposite, from outside to outside.

PUTTING

A few years ago, when Jack Burke and I were next-door neighbors, I often went to his kitchen for an early-morning cup of coffee and a chat. I'll never forget the Monday morning when I complained to him how poorly I'd putted in the just-completed tournament. "Well, let's go fix it," Jack said. "No time like the present." We left our steaming mugs on the table and drove straight to Champions.

The putting green was covered with dew, and the sun was barely peeking through the trees. I had my putter and a handful of practice balls. "Right here," Jack said, pointing to a spot about fifteen feet from a hole. I dropped the balls, stroked the first putt, and boom, right in the heart. The ball traced a path through the dew from where I stood to the cup.

And with that, Jack walked away. "When you make another one on that exact same line, come and get me," he called over his shoulder. "I'm gonna go get a cup of coffee."

In the next hour, I confirmed the point that Jack was so obviously and dramatically making. Though I holed many more putts before the sun got above the trees and burned off the dew, rarely did any two putts follow the same precise line to the hole. The lesson for me then and for you now is this: We're too often preoccupied with line. The weight of the hit—distance—is more crucial. As the lines in the dew confirmed for me, the hole opens up for putts from many different directions.

Putting is often overlooked, but I have never seen anything lower your score like making a few putts.

Before we talk about technique, consider a factor that is often just as important: attitude. When sports psychologist Bob Rotella gives a speech, he often tells his audience an anecdote about my mental approach to putting Riviera in the '95 PGA. The greens were new, spike marks loomed like little trees to some players, and complaints were frequent. But I looked at those greens and said, "Perfect." On perfectly smooth surfaces of unbroken green, I sometimes find it harder to putt. So at Riviera, *I used the spike marks as targets, not as obstacles.* I proved that you can make putts on a green that is a little rough—if you think you can.

Many of the fundamentals of full shots also apply to putting.

One fundamental, however, is different. The putter should be gripped with both thumbs down the shaft. This keeps the palms opposing, which helps keep the putter face square. Especially if you use the right arm stroke, you'll want the palm of the right hand to be flush against the handle. The most popular putting grip—and the grip I use—is the reverse overlap.

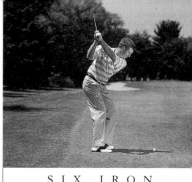

SIX IRON

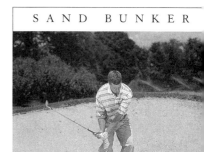

SAND BUNKER

Simply put the index finger of the left hand over the fingers of the right hand. It's a very comfortable grip for putting.

Realize first that every putt is straight; the green does the breaking. So you must putt to the high point, the spot from which your ball will roll into the hole. That's your target, not the hole.

Once you have your target in mind, you must decide which power source to apply to hit the putt. You have really only two choices: the right arm stroke or the shoulder stroke. Use one or the other; it's not effective to combine the two.

Try to hole each putt when practicing, then move on to a different putt.

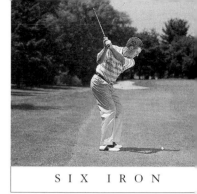

SIX IRON

In the **arm stroke**, the right arm should dominate. The left hand and shoulders are out of it. On the backswing, the right elbow bends, and on the downswing the right elbow straightens. Jack Nicklaus's piston-like arm stroke demonstrates that this is a method that can work very well. I played all of '93 and '94 with an arm stroke and won the Australian Open with it. But I've found in recent years that I'm more consistent with a shoulder stroke.

The **shoulder stroke** is the most popular on the Tour. Recall the chipping technique described earlier. This stroke is basically the same, with unmoving wrists, and power provided by lowering the left shoulder on the backswing and raising it on the downswing.

SAND BUNKER

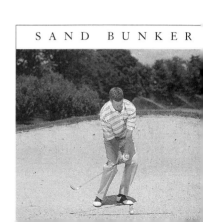

141

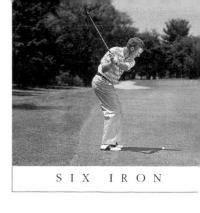

The winning putt, the 1995 PGA at Riviera, Los Angeles. Elkington made sure not to completely surrender to celebration, because Colin Montgomerie still had a putt to tie.

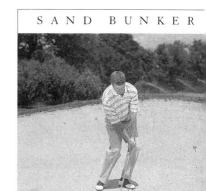

THE GOLFER'S WORKOUT

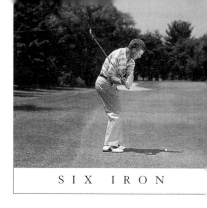

SIX IRON

Like most champions of the modern era, Steve Elkington pursues many paths to his goal of winning golf tournaments. Mastery of the five fundamentals, competent instruction, mental and emotional balance, and practice—each is part of the equation.

Another increasingly important element in the professional golfer's life is fitness. It hasn't always been so.

Almost alone among golfers forty years ago, Gary Player stretched and lifted weights and watched what he ate, pushing his body to improve his performance. Despite his proselytizing and his success, not many of his peers thought it was worth the effort.

"I regarded golf as an athletic pursuit while most of my contemporaries revelled in the minimal physical demand they felt it imposed on them," Player wrote in *To Be the Best* (1991). "[They] argued that the swing itself was the best exercise for the game and that a hectic nocturnal social life was no serious handicap."

Those days are no more. Champion golfers justifiably con-

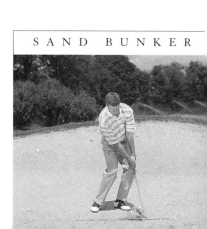

SAND BUNKER

sider themselves to be athletes, and a fitness van follows the U.S. PGA Tour from city to city. Elkington never labored under the misconception that hoisting a barbell leads inevitably to a musclebound disaster of a golf swing. "I realized that working out was important the first time I saw Greg Norman, back in the mid-'80s," Elkington says. "Flexibility throughout the round—and strength at the end of the round—that's why you work out.

I got organized with my training in 1991. I built good habits, but I was to discover that I wasn't focusing enough on the golf muscles."

That changed when he got hurt. That's when he met Russ Paine.

Paine, forty-two, Administrator of HealthSouth Sports Medicine and Rehabilitation Center in Houston, may be the most respected physical therapist in the world of professional athletics. His clients include well-known baseball, basketball, and football players as well as little-known astronauts; he's the rehabilitation consultant to the Houston Rockets and to NASA. When in late 1996 Elkington's right hip began to hurt so much that he could hardly swing, he went to see Dr. Frank Jobe, the orthopedic surgeon who consults for the PGA Tour. Jobe sent Elkington to Paine.

"Weakness in the gluteus medius and the hip flexor," says Paine, a Jean-Claude Van Damme look-alike whose road to major-league baseball (he was a pitcher) was blocked by the surgeon's knife. "Those are the muscles to the side and the front of the hip. Because he's ligamentously lax—'loose-jointed,' as your grandmother might say—and because he hits so many golf balls, Steve needed a lot of strengthening in that area. The hip is a critical area, with forces meeting from above and below and causing a lot of stress.

"Steve's case reminds us that there are two big reasons for working out. First, you want more strength and endurance to hit longer, better shots. Second and more important, you want to prevent injuries in practice and in play."

Although golf isn't usually viewed as a vigorous sport, it's certainly not a benign activity, according to Paine. "About sixty-two percent of golfers get injured every year. Injuries to the back, the left wrist, and left elbow are the most frequent; the hips, shoulders, and hands are hurt less often."

To measure the golf swing's physical stresses exactly, Paine, his colleague Ron M. Johnson, and other physical therapists wired scores of test subjects. Intramuscularly implanted fine-wire electrodes were connected to computer monitors whose digital readouts showed which muscles are the most active in the swing. Motion-analysis programs using multiple high-speed cameras revealed muscle firing patterns. From sub-scapularis to trapezius to latissimus dorsi, the researchers could now tell precisely what was happening beneath the golfer's skin when he or she swings a club.

"One big conclusion was that golfers are weakest in the abs," says Paine. "Back injuries are common, and debilitating, but golfers are usually pretty strong in the back. Weak abdominals deserve much more of the blame. The muscles in the front—the abdominals, the obliques, and the rectus—wrap around the torso. They help control the spinal curve and the rotation of the trunk.

"You're bent over in everything you do in the golf swing, and you're always rotating around the spine. That's why it's critical to build the muscles that support the spinal column."

The electromyographic analysis also showed the danger of stiffness. Inflexible golfers not only lose the ball-hitting bene-fits of proper swing fundamentals, they also tend to hurt

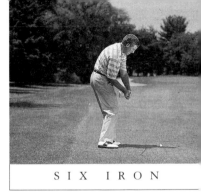

SIX IRON

SAND BUNKER

themselves, especially in the lower back. Golfers with tight hamstrings, for example, often compensate by bending forward too much. And another back bites the dust.

"The goal of our research was to discover an efficient workout for the golfer. Let's not have you go to the gym and try to bench-press three hundred pounds over and over. Instead, you can gain a mechanical advantage and prevent injury by using the drills described here. They're the same exercises Steve uses."

PAINE'S CONDITIONING AND training exercises are based on these principles; the first two are most important:

- Muscular strength and flexibility depend on each other. Strength without flexibility is almost useless.
- Correct posture and a stable base must be established for optimal arm swing. The muscles that support the posture and base are those surrounding the hips, spine, abdomen, and shoulders.
- The golfer should condition the entire body, not just the upper body. Energy and leverage in the golf swing are delivered from the legs and hips, as well as the trunk, arms, and shoulders.
- Muscles should be trained as they function during the swing. For example, the large muscles of the arms and chest (the latissimus dorsi and the pectoralis major) act as accelerators, while the rotator cuff and scapular muscles in the shoulder work primarily to stabilize and decelerate. Since the muscles have different jobs to do in the swing, they should not be exercised the same way.

SIX IRON

- The arms should be trained to act in concert with the leg, hip, and trunk muscles.
- The golfer must train for bilateral strength. Both left and right sides of the body contribute to the golf swing.
- Muscular strength should be emphasized in the workout before dynamic strength and power. In other words, you need to develop a baseline of static strength before beginning drills that enhance swinging power.
- Conditioning and training should be done year-round. To avoid overtraining, injury, and boredom, the workouts should be varied.

To vary the workout, Paine recommends dividing your golf year into three periods: in-season, off-season, and preparation. These divisions allow the golfer to peak athletically at a desired time and prevent over- or undertraining.

In-season exercise should have relatively few repetitions but high intensity. Off-season drill should be just the reverse—high volume, low intensity. In the preparation phase, four to six weeks before the start of the season, volume and intensity should be moderate.

THE GOLFER'S WORKOUT has four parts. Even the routine outlined here for the half hour before you tee off has the basics of warm-up, stretching, and strengthening. The fourth component, cardiovascular exercise adequate to induce a little heavy breathing, will probably not be achieved on the practice tee.

Warm-up literally raises the temperature of the body tissues. Five to ten minutes of brisk walking, slow jogging, stair

SAND BUNKER

stepping, or riding the stationary bicycle will increase blood flow, viscosity of joint fluids, heart rate, perspiration, and deep muscle temperature. Now you're ready to stretch.

Stretching increases flexibility and reduces strains, sprains, and soreness. To stretch effectively, Paine reminds his clients to:

- Warm up first.
- Begin each stretch slowly and smoothly.
- Breathe normally throughout the stretch. Exhale fully when moving further into a stretch.
- Concentrate. Feel each stretch.
- Never strain or force a stretch into a painful range.
- Hold each stretch for twenty or thirty seconds. Do not bounce!
- Repeat each stretch three to five times. The greatest improvement in flexibility takes place in the first four stretches.
- Never stretch in a recently injured area, or if you feel a sharp pain.
- Stretch, after warm-up in order: hamstrings, calves, hip flexors, back, and posterior shoulder.

Paine presents two **strengthening** programs, one for recreational golfers, the other for the player willing to work for optimal condition and performance. The goals of both are to gradually increase strength and general fitness.

Moderate weights are used in three or four sets of ten to twelve repetitions. The final set should be difficult to achieve with proper form; when this final set is easy, add more weight.

Cardiovascular conditioning should elevate the heart rate for twenty minutes three to five times per week. In addition to increasing energy while playing golf, this sort of training can quickly enhance general fitness.

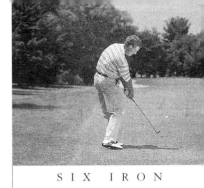

SIX IRON

EACH OF THE THREE workouts outlined here should take thirty to forty-five minutes.

Refer to the photos and captions for specific exercises.

THE GOLFER'S WORKOUT

- ■ Warm-up
- ■ Stretch
- ■ Trunk/abdominals obliques, rectus abdominus, and lower abdominals
- ■ Scapular muscles: seated rows
- ■ Shoulder/rotator cuff: dumbbell forward flexion, empty can, and deceleration
- ■ Repeat daily for three days, rest for one day, repeat

THE GOLFER'S ADVANCED WORKOUT

- ■ Warm-up
- ■ Stretch
- ■ Day 1: Trunk/abdominals, chest, shoulders
  - • Trunk
    - • Obliques
    - • Rectus abdominus and lower abdominals
    - • Upper and lower abdominals with plyoball
    - • Side-to-side plyoball
    - • Plyoball throw and catch

SAND BUNKER

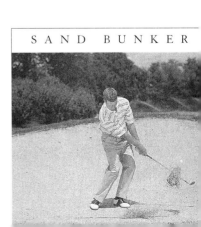

151

- Chest
  - Dumbbell bench press
- Shoulders/rotator cuff
  - Dumbbell forward flexion
  - Dumbbell empty can
  - Dumbbell deceleration
- ■ Day 2: Hips/legs, scapular muscles
  - Hips/legs
    - Hip abduction—lying on side
    - Hip abduction—standing
    - Hip extension—standing
    - Hip flexion—supine
    - Hip internal and external rotation
  - Scapular muscles/latissimus dorsi
    - Seated rows
    - Pulldowns
- ■ Day 3: Rest
- ■ Day 4: Repeat Day 1
- ■ Day 5: Repeat Day 2

PRE-GOLF WARM-UP ROUTINE

- ■ Walk briskly to the practice range or putting green
- ■ Standing low back and hamstring stretch (figure 4)
- ■ Lumbar extension stretch (figure 5)
- ■ Standing shoulder rotation stretch with golf club
- ■ Posterior cuff stretch (figure 14a)
- ■ Begin hitting balls, progressing from short to long irons, to three wood, to driver

Figure 1   Warm-up
Proper warm-up allows muscle temperature to rise, which will allow stretching to proceed with enhanced results.

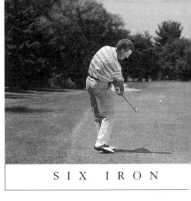

SIX   IRON

Figure 2
Piriformis stretch
This stretch allows the hip rotators to stretch. This muscle group tends to tighten during the golf swing.

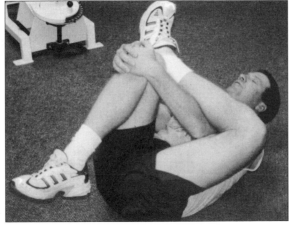

Figure 3
Hip flexor stretch
This stretch lengthens the hip flexors, which often become overtightened and fatigued in the golfer.

SAND   BUNKER

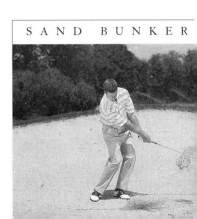

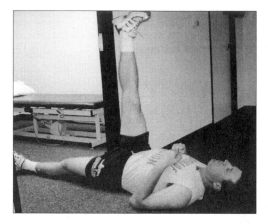

Figure 4   Hamstring stretches
Hamstring stretching is an extremely important golf stretch. If the hamstrings are tight, pelvic movement will be limited. If pelvic movement is limited at ball address, increased lumbar spine flexion is required to address the ball.

(a) Hold this position for 20 seconds.

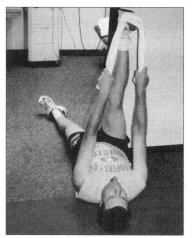

(b) A more aggressive stretch can be performed by keeping the leg straight as in (a) and by using a towel to pull the leg away from the wall. Keep the knee straight!

(c) As you can see, I don't have a problem with tight hamstrings!

(d) I'd like to see the seniors do this!

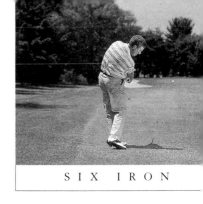

SIX   IRON

Figure 5   Lumbar extension stretch
This stretch is a must to prevent back injuries. This stretch, combined with lumbar strengthening, will help avoid a leading cause of early golf retirement—back pain.

SAND   BUNKER

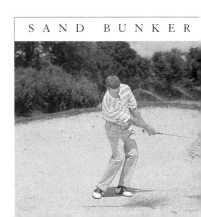

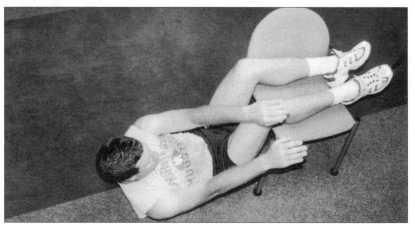

Figure 6 a, b   Oblique abdominals
The obliques are extremely important in rotating the trunk through the impact zone. If you have laid off golf for a while and play a round of golf, these muscles should be sore along their insertion onto the ribs. Reach and hold for two seconds, alternating left and right. (Note: Keep your low back flat on the floor to stabilize the pelvis.)

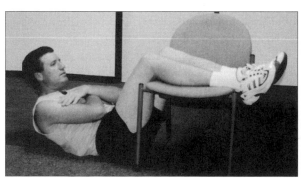

**Figure 6 c
Rectus abdominus,** or straight abdominal workout. Keep pelvis flat, reach and touch or cross arms as shown. Hold for two to three seconds and repeat.

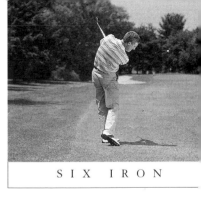

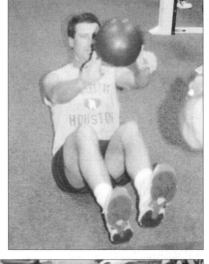

Figure 7 a, b   Plyoball sit-ups
For this exercise, use a weighted ball (15-pound ball shown) while keeping heels off ground as you catch, then throw ball back to workout partner.

Figure 7 c
Advanced trunk strengthening is provided as workout partner tosses the 15-pound plyoball to you and you catch and throw to emphasize trunk rotator strengthening.

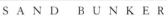

Figure 8   Lower abdominal routine
Advanced strengthening of lower abdominals is provided as partner throws your legs toward the ground. Golfer decelerates this motion using abdominals—allowing heels to reach within two inches of the ground, then returning to start position.

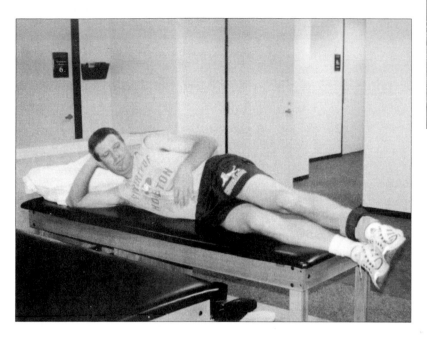

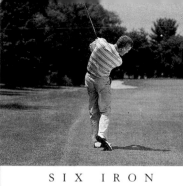

S I X   I R O N

Figure 9 a, b   Hip abductor strengthening
The hip abductor muscle is extremely important in preventing lateral sliding of the hips.
Simply lift leg away from body, slowly lower leg to start position, and repeat.

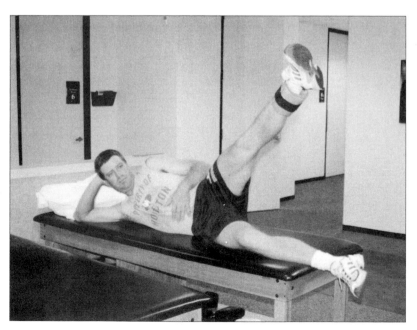

S A N D   B U N K E R

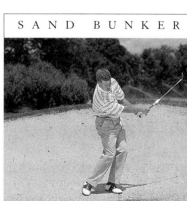

Figure 10 a, b
Advanced hip abductor routine
Using a Theraband or a cable column,
perform same motion as Figure 9 a, b.

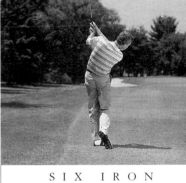

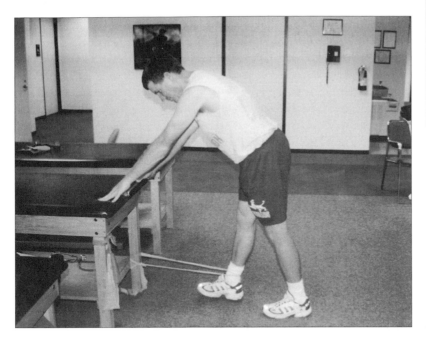

Figure 11 a, b   Hip extensor strengthening

Maintain trunk position as hip is extended away from body. Return to start position and repeat.

S A N D   B U N K E R

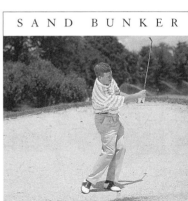

Figure 12 a, b   Hip flexor strengthening
The hip flexor tends to become overlengthened in golfers with hypermobile (loose) joints.
Using a Theraband or elastic tubing, pull knee to chest using hip muscles.

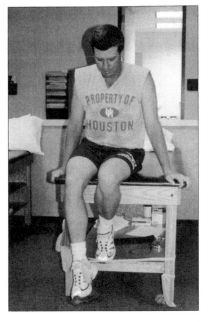 

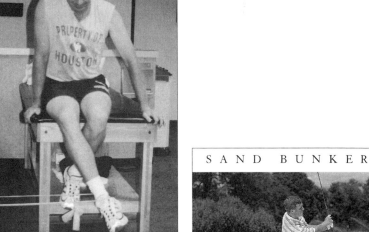

S I X   I R O N

Figure 13 a, b   Hip internal rotation using theraband
The hip rotators are very important in stabilizing the lateral slide. Backswing forces are more concentrated on the back leg, so this leg should be emphasized during strengthening.

Figure 13 c
Hip external rotation
Same activity as
Figure 13 a, b—opposite motion.

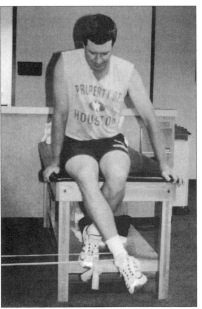

S A N D   B U N K E R

Figure 14 a   Posterior (back) cuff stretch
Very important warm-up for rotator cuff. Pull arm across body, hold for ten seconds, and
repeat ten times.

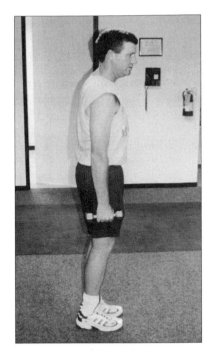

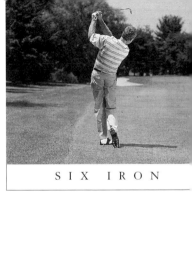

S I X   I R O N

Figure 15 a, b
Forward flexion using dumbbell
Start with a 1- to 3-pound dumbbell.
Elevate arm just above horizontal, hold
two to three seconds, and slowly lower.

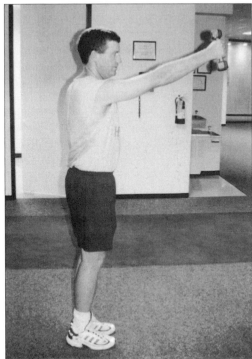

S A N D   B U N K E R

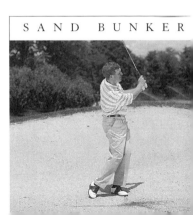

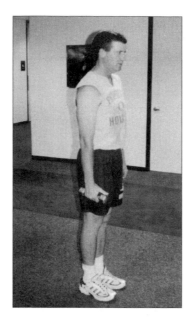 

Figure 16 a, b, c, d   Emptying can exercise
Begin with arm to side, thumb up. Lift arm up at an angle 30 degrees from horizontal. Pause at the top, then begin to empty can as thumb is pointed downward, while slowly lowering arm.

 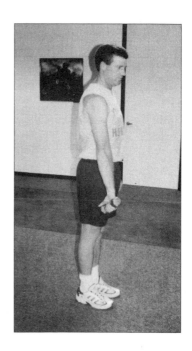

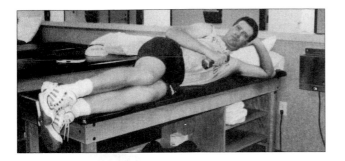

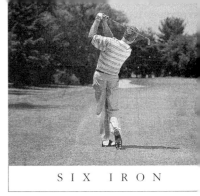

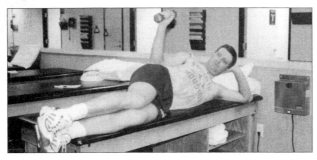

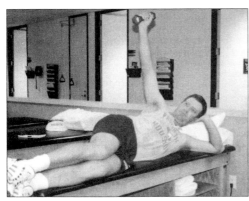

Figure 17 a, b, c, d
Deceleration
This exercise strengthens the posterior cuff. Begin with elbow to side (a), rotate backwards (b), lift arm to ceiling (c), then slowly lower across chest towards floor (d).

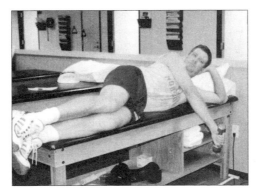

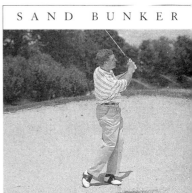

Figure 18   Seated rows
Technique is important here. Reach forward to begin (a). Pull handle into chest while keeping elbows tucked to sides; pinch and hold shoulder blades while protruding chest (b). Reach to start position and return.

ELK'S RECORD

EXEMPT STATUS
Winner, 1995 PGA Championship

JUNIOR GOLF
Winner, 1980 Australia–New Zealand Amateur
Winner, 1981 Doug Sanders Junior World Championship

COLLEGE
University of Houston (1985)
Two-time All-American
Two-time individual Southwest Conference Champion
Two-time NCAA team champion

TURNED PRO
1985

FINISHED Q SCHOOL
1986

JOINED TOUR
1987

MAJOR VICTORIES
1995 PGA Championship

TOUR VICTORIES
1990 Kmart Greater Greensboro Open
1991 The Players Championship
1992 Infiniti Tournament of Champions
1994 Buick Southern Open
1995 Mercedes Championship, PGA Championship
1997 Doral-Ryder Open, The Players Championship

NON-TOUR WINS
1993 Fred Meyer Challenge, with Tom Purtzer
1993 Shark Shoot-Out, with Raymond Floyd
1995 Shark Shoot-Out, with Mark Calcaveccia

INTERNATIONAL VICTORIES
1992 Australian Open (Australia)
1996 Honda Invitational (Asia)

NATIONAL TEAMS
1994, 1996 Presidents Cup
1994 World Cup
1994, 1995, 1996 Dunhill Cup

Annie and Sam Elkington

THE JOURNEY

As you journey through life,
Choose your destinations well
but do not hurry to get there
You'll arrive soon enough
Wander the back roads and forgotten paths
Keeping the destination in your heart,
like a fixed point on a compass
Seek out new voices, strange sights, and
ideas foreign to your own
Such things enrich the soul
If, upon arrival,
you find that your destination is not exactly as you
dreamed,
do not be disappointed
Think instead of all you would have missed
And know that the true worth of your travel
lies not in where you are at journey's end,
but in who you came to be along the way.

I was a boy who dreamed of winning a major championship
as a man I fulfilled my dream
But it isn't the trophy I value as much as the journey
and the people on the journey:
everyone I've met who shared a joke, a story, advice, a beer
You are the ones who have made me what I am,
and I am deeply grateful
My mother, my father, and my brother Robert never told me I
couldn't do it
"Reach for the stars" they said;
Lisa, my wife, who I feel I have loved my whole life;
Annie and Sam, my two beautiful children.
The best part is that we get to journey together for a long
time to come.

—Elk

ILLUSTRATION CREDITS

INDEX